TRAVEL
WEST CARIBBEAN

Travel Book & Photo Album

CHELSEA KONG

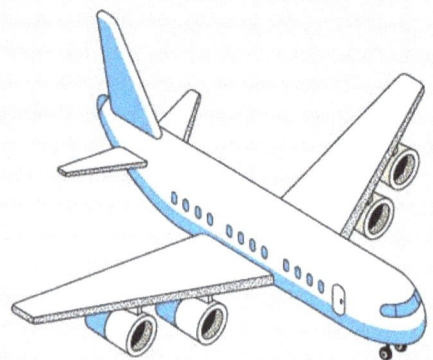

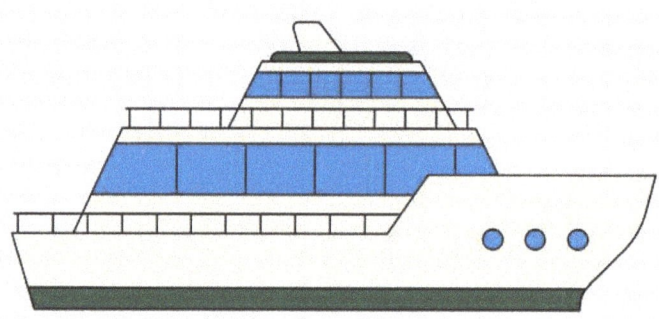

Printed in 2023-2025, Made in Toronto, Canada
ISBN: 978-1-990399-87-9
Other Paperback: 978-1-998335-01-5

Caribbean mood

Travel onboard Freedom of the Seas

Explore West Caribbean

KNOW YOUR BUDGET BEFORE YOU BOOK YOUR CRUISE VACATION. YOU CAN REGISTER FOR MEMBERSHIP.

ROYAL CARIBBEAN

FREEDOM OF THE SEAS

Book your cruise first!
Get it on sale.

Travel on a cruise boat

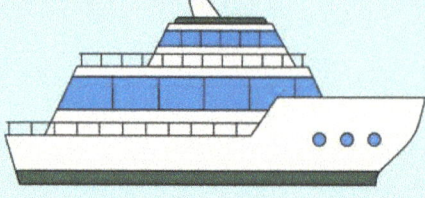

CRUISE: SEPTEMBER 8-15, 2024
CHECK-IN: JULY 25, 2024

TRAVEL DESIGN CRUISE HOLIDAY

Let us take you on a journey of a lifetime. Your adventure begins here!

OUR SERVICES

- Flight Reservations
- Hotel Reservations
- Tour Packages
- Cruise Reservations
- Car Rental

安利遊輪假期
www.traveldesigncruises.com

PRICE START AT

$576 USD

+310.803.7050   www.traveldesignusa.com

BOOK NOW

Interior Room

Choose your room based on your budget.
The lower priced rooms are interior and
located towards the back of the ship.
Midship interior rooms are nice if
you can spend a little more money.
If you can afford, get an ocean view room.

Explore the World

ORGANIZE YOUR TRIP WITH US!

CHECK DETAILS TO ENSURE ACCURACY.
THE PASSPORT MUST BE VALID FOR AT
LEAST 6 MONTHS BEFORE YOU TRAVEL.

travel itinerary

DAY 1 — Ft. Lauderdale, Florida

BUDGET

PLACE TO SEE

DAY 2 — At Sea

BUDGET

PLACE TO SEE

DAY 3 — George Town, Grand Cayman

BUDGET

PLACE TO SEE

DAY 4 — Falmouth, Jamaica

BUDGET

PLACE TO SEE

DAY 5 — Nassau, Bahamas

BUDGET

PLACE TO SEE

Itinerary changes can happen anytime and your cruise line will email you. They will inform you about excursions being refunded. New excursions should be available for booking.

travel
itinerary

DAY 6

Perfect Day at CocoCay, Bahamas

BUDGET

PLACE TO SEE

PASSPORT

DAY 7

At Sea

BUDGET

PLACE TO SEE

DAY 8

Ft. Lauderdale, Florida

BUDGET

PLACE TO SEE

My Travel Planner

Destination

Transportation

Date & time

Hotel

Places to Visit

Budget Estimation

Notes

NOTES

_____

_____

_____

_____

_____

_____

_____

_____

IMPORTANT

_____

_____

_____

_____

_____

_____

To Do List

_____

_____

_____

_____

_____

@reallygreatsite

CHOOSE YOUR EXCURSIONS

BOOK DURING BLACK FRIDAY IF POSSIBLE AND IN ADVANCE TO GET THE BEST DEALS.

FORT LAUDERDALE

START YOUR TRIP A DAY EARLIER!

Book your hotel and transportation.
Avoid flight delays and other issues.

EVERGLADES AIRBOAT RIDE
JUNGLE QUEEN RIVERBOAT
WATER TAXI

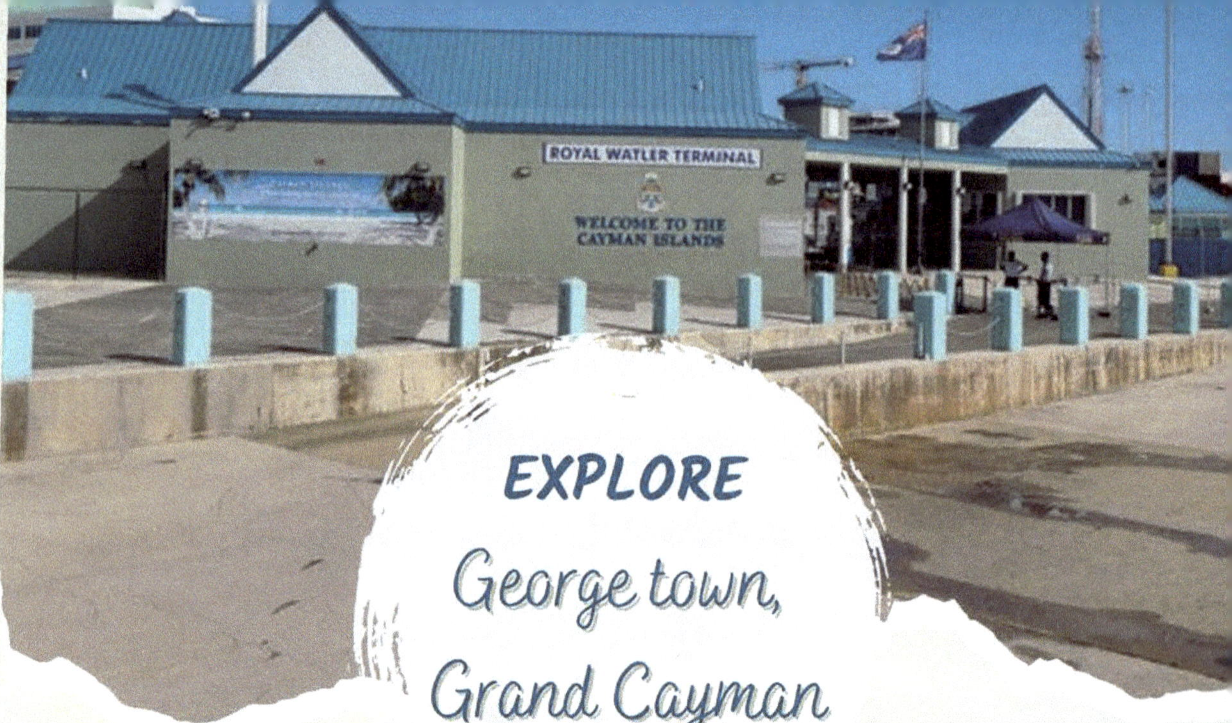

EXPLORE
George town, Grand Cayman

STINGRAY CITY
STARFISH POINT BEACH
DOLPHINS
TURTLE ENCOUNTER
BLOWHOLE AND
LIGHTHOUSE
SEVEN MILE BEACH
SANDBAR
CORAL BEACH
SNORKELING
CANMANA BAY

KONOKO FALLS

DOLPHIN COVE

FALMOUTH, JAMAICA

DUNN'S RIVER FALLS

BOTANNICAL GARDEN

GREEN GROTTO CAVES

ORCHO RIOS

SHIPMATE APP HAS EXCURSIONS.

FALMOUTH, JAMAICA

Cayman Islands
Ocho Rios
Blue Waters Beach
Montego Bay

Hell
Wave Jet Tour
Flight Line

NASSAU, BAHAMAS

Seaworld Explorer

Baha Bay Water Park

Blue Lagoon Island Shark Encounter

Nassau Sail & Reef Snorkeling

Pearl Island Beach Escape

New Providence Sightseeing Tour

NASSAU, BAHAMAS

Atlantis Dolphin Cay Playtime

A FUN TIME INTERACTING WITH A DOLPHIN AND YOU GET FULL ACCESS TO AQAVENTURE WHICH INCLUDES ALL OF THE ADVENTURES THAT IS OFFERED BY ATLANTIS PARADISE ISLAND RESORT.

Atlantis Aquaventure Waterpark

THIS IS THE FAMOUS ATLANTIS PARADISE ISLAND RESORT AND AQUATIC ADVENTURE. ENJOY A DAY PASS AND FULL ACCESS TO AMENITIES. IT HAS 5 MILES OF BEAUTIFUL BEACHES AND LAGOONS.

Nassau Jeep Adventure

BOOK AN EXCURSION RIDE IN A JEEP WRANGLER THAT BRINGS YOU TO HISTORICAL PLACES. THERE WILL BE SAMPLES OF LOCAL DELIGHTS AND A BAHAMIAN JUNKANOO EXPERIENCE. YOU CAN ALSO EXPLORE MORE EXPERIENCES.

MORE TO SEE

There are more tours and activities that you can do here, but these are the ones offered by Royal Caribbean. Check out Fort Charlotte and Fort Montagu. You can also take a fishing tour. You can also enjoy the cabanas.

Harbour Island

THERE IS MORE TO ENJOY AT HARBOUR ISLAND. YOU CAN ALSO VISIT COLONIAL DUNMORE, PINK SANDS, ELEUTHRA. TAKE A HARBOUR ISLAND TOUR. THEY ARE KNOWN FOR THE CONCH. THERE IS A PLACE CALLED QUEEN CONCH.

PERFECT DAY COCOCAY, BAHAMAS

CocoCay has many activities that you can do without cost. There are beautiful beaches and water. They have a Thrill Water Park, zip lining, and every water sport you can imagine.

CocoCay, Bahamas

Splashaway Bay	South Beach
Captain Jill's	Sports Courts
Galleon	Fitness Classes
Skipper's Grill	Freshwater
Chill Grill	showers
Snack Shack	Tram service
Oasis Lagoon pool	Cabanas
Chill Island	

SHIPMATE

THIS APP WILL GIVE YOU ACCESS TO OTHER CRUISES TO CONSIDER.

CHECK THIS APP FOR ADDITIONAL EXCURSIONS AND SERVICES.

EXCURSIONS

Book in advance and print the eticket that they send to your email.

CRUISE SHIP

You can see your cruises and access the itinerary.

PORTS

This will give you the different ports destinations.

Choose wisely

Keep in mind that you can only book one excursion a day usually, unless they are short. You will need time to travel to each one and to get back to the cruise ship. They expect you to be there in the evening. They will be leaving the Cruise Port to travel to the next destination. Download the maps before your vacation to save on your phone. Read cruise's blog for tips.

If you went on the cruise line website. You need to add the booking confirmation number. The website will add all your details, including any booked excursions. Review the policies for your cruise line. They are mandatory to enjoy your cruise vacation. You will be removed from the cruise if you don't. They won't compensate you and you will have to change your booking plans. Make sure you stay updated by checking the App every month up to the time of your cruise. They may add additional details on the app during the cruise. Check in on the app on the date provided. It will guide you to what to do before and during the cruise. You will see Day 1 of the itinerary starts at 6am. They have a daily planner with activities that you can register for at a cost. The app asks you to add the calendar after you board. The app has everything you need.

You can still book more excursions prior to boarding the ship, but it is best to get them when they are on sale, especially if you are not a citizen of the USA because of the exchange rate. Ask your cruise line questions to find out more details about your cruise. You need to make sure you aren't missing anything. As a first time cruiser, you don't want to be last to board or to have other issues happen. Cruise lines can deny or delay passengers who do not comply to the rules. Your luggage is another issue that they can delay or accidentally leave behind. Plan ahead and prepare for any unexpected situations. Keep in mind there are many other passengers boarding. Royal Caribbean Blog on YouTube is beneficial to help you be more prepared. The inside cabins on the ship are small, so you have limited space available. Find out more about your cabin before your vacation. Keep your valuables safe. Call the Excursions desk for details on your excursion. You will notice when connected to the ship's Wi-Fi.

YOU CAN RECEIVE MESSAGES, EMAILS, ETC, BUT YOU CAN'T EMAIL OR ACCESS SITES. YOU CAN'T VIEW YOUR WHATSAPP MESSAGES OR ANY NOTIFICATIONS ON OTHER APPS. IT WILL GIVE YOU NOTIFICATIONS, BUT WILL NOT ALLOW YOU TO READ ALL OF THEM. IT ONLY LETS YOU ACCESS CERTAIN ONES TO READ EVEN WHEN THEY LEAK THROUGH THE NETWORK. FACEBOOK MESSAGES AND NOTIFICATIONS WILL POP UP, BUT YOU WON'T BE ABLE TO VIEW ON THE APP. MESSENGER MAY BE AVAILABLE, BUT YOU CAN'T SEND MESSAGES OUT. SIGNAL MESSAGES ALSO CAN BE ACCESSED AND RECEIVED. YOU CAN ONLY CHECK THE CRUISE APP. IF YOU HAVE A US PLAN, YOU WILL ONLY HAVE ACCESS TO THE NETWORK WHEN YOU ARE IN FLORIDA. YOU WILL NEED TO REMEMBER TO CHANGE TO FLIGHT MODE AND TURN ON WI-FI TO AVOID ROAMING CHARGES. THE WEATHER IS HOT AND YOUR PHONE HAS TO BE ABLE TO ENDURE THE HEAT, SALT WATER, AND WATER.

Do your research before you travel. It's good to know the places that you are going to visit during the cruise in case you only want to do a few excursions. You need to budget for several months. Learn to snorkel ahead of time if you plan to do that excursion. If you work, book the vacation time is off with them too. Make sure you met the vaccination requirements. The cruise may require you to complete a form. In most cases, Covid is over and they should not require it.

THINGS TO DO

- BOOK ACCOMMODATION
- TRAVEL INSURANCE
- BOOK TRANSPORTATION
- SEAT RESERVATION FOR DINNER ON THE CRUISE.
- STAY CONNECTED WITH TRAVEL AGENT
- CHECK THE CRUISE LINE APP.

- RESEARCH AND BRING MAPS
- PACK TRAVEL ITINERARY
- RENT A CAR IS NEEDED
- WIFI ACCESS
- CHECK APPS
- PROOF OF VACCINATION

Buy what you need on Boxing Day and then spring to summer sales. You can shop for additional items you need. You need 2 swim suits, suitable sandals or multi-use travel slippers, dress shoes, formal wear, purse, swim cardigan, pantyhose, and waterproof products. Set a budget to spend for all the items you need to purchase. You must dress properly for the formal nights. You may also want a travel purse. You should have a flat phone case for the waterproof bag.

BEST ITEMS FOR PACKING

THERE ARE LUGGAGE BAGS THAT FIT FOR EVERY AIRLINE. IT IS IDEAL TO CHOOSE LUGGAGE FOR THE AIRLINE THAT YOU USE MOST. TRAVEL BACKPACKS ARE LIGHT PERSONAL ITEMS THAT FIT UNDER YOUR SEAT ON THE PLANE. THEY CAN HOLD ELECTRONICS AND MANY IMPORTANT ITEMS. THEY HAVE A WATERPROOF POCKET. YOU CAN GET ONE WITH A USB CHARGING CABLE HOLDER. GET A LIGHT PACKABLE RAINCOAT. USE A TRAVEL WALLET, TSA LOCK, TSA-FRIENDLY TRAVEL BOTTLES, A MAGNETIC HAT CLIP TO PUT ON YOUR BACKPACK, A COLLAPSIBLE WATER BOTTLE, COMPRESSOR SOCKS, KEY JEWELRY PIECES, THIN COMPACT PILLOW YOU CAN ROLL OR FOLD FLAT, AND 2 IN 1 STRAIGHTENER/CURLING IRON, TRAVEL STEAMER, AND INTERNATIONAL TRAVEL ADAPTER.

You need to roll some items and flatten others to save room. Wear new or gently used clothing only. You can pack clothes in ziplocks and label them for each day of the week. You could buy packing cubes which hold more items and may come with laundry bags. A space-saving laundry bag is good for the dirty laundry. When you pack, limit certain items and use all the space at the bottom of the luggage. You need to maximize on the space available. Pack the heavy items on bottom and light items on top. Bring extra undergarments. Wear bulky shoes on the plane instead of packing in the luggage. Keep all liquids together. All electronics should be easily accessible to remove from a bag at security check.

It is recommended that you bring lightweight shoes when you travel. In my case, I got formal dress shoes, water shoes, Comfortwear orthotic shoes, flat foldable travel slippers, and flat sandals. You will need the appropriate footwear for each occasion. You may not require water shoes. It depends on the excursions you do. Comfortwear shoes are great for individuals with feet issues. They are comfortable and help protect your feet. It can relieve or help to recover from feet issues. Get what you need for keeping your laundry clean. Keep in mind your clothes etc will be soiled as there are no laundry facilities available. Disposable underwear is ideal if you don't want dirty undies in your luggage. You will also have to manage the smell.

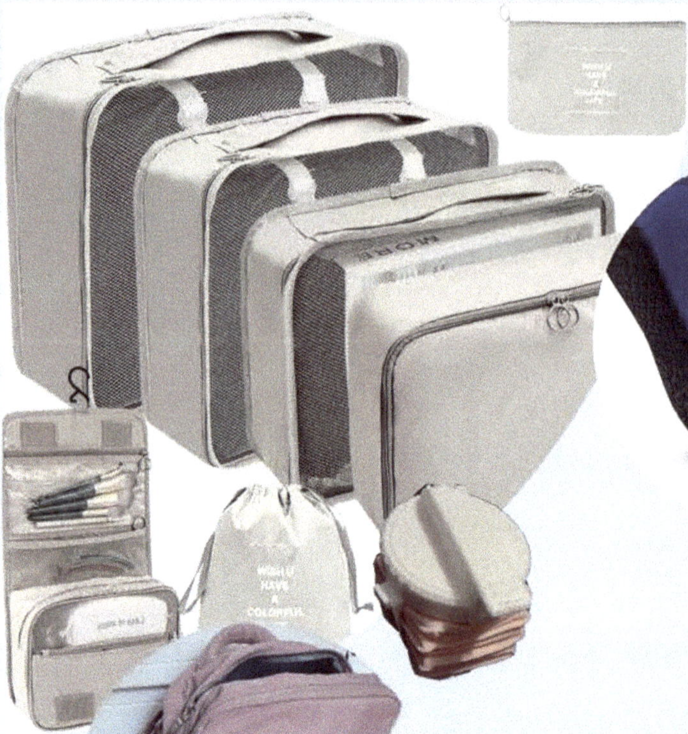

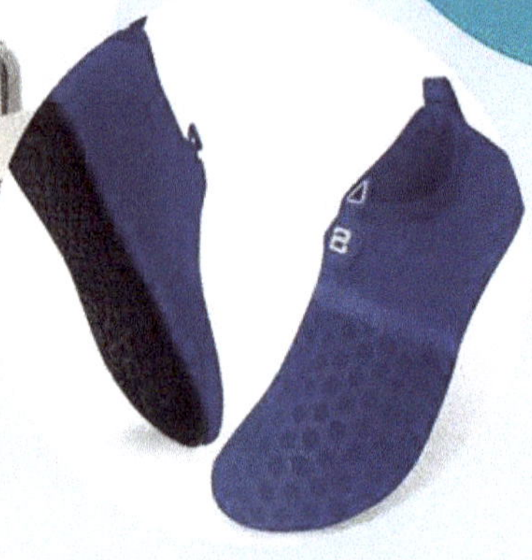

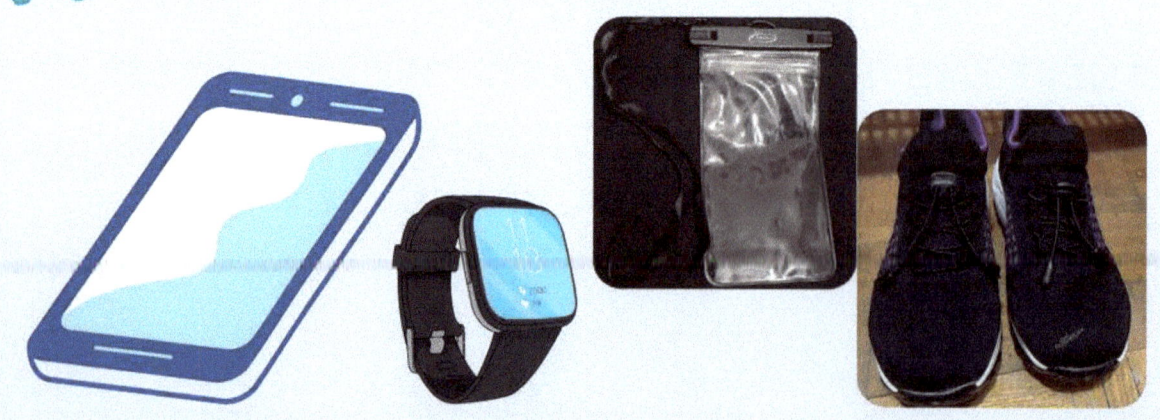

WATERPROOF AND LIGHT

OTHER ITEMS TO CONSIDER

If you like cosmetics, you will need a travel kit for your beauty products. This will go in the checked baggage since you can only have 100ml liquids in the ziplock or water proof liquids bag. Saran Wrap will protect from leaks. Consider your hygiene and beauty kit. Get a small travel kit size. A compact blanket will be good in fall and winter. You can also get a travel stroller. If you enjoy reading, then the Kindle device is ideal for travel or a mini-iPad as long as it's light. Use cable ties, and electronic travel organizer. Pack as light as possible. Get a waterproof cover for your camera, cable clips, and a portable battery charger. Keep electronics in your personal item.

Search for the best flights to book 5 months in advance to your cruise vacation.

ALLOW YOURSELF ENOUGH TIME WHEN YOU ARRIVE TO REACH THE CRUISE PORT (FLIGHT AT 7AM). IF YOU ARRIVE A DAY EARLIER, PLAN YOUR WELL WHERE TO STAY FOR THE NIGHT AND GET FAMILIAR WITH THE LOCATION. YOU SHOULD BE AT FT. LAUDERDALE BY 11AM. KEEP IN MIND YOU NEED TO BE CHECKED IN BEFORE 1PM.

📍 AIRPORTS

You can choose either Fort Lauderdale–Hollywood International Airport or Miami Airport. There are hotels nearby and both have shuttle service from the airport to the cruise port. There may be a charge depending on where you stay. Research the airport details so you know what is available, where to go, and what to expect. Be there early at the security. Check your boarding pass. If your boarding pass shows "S's", it means an extra security check. You need to allow extra time before boarding.

Book flight

Departure: 10:15am-1:15pm
Return 2:05-5:05pm
Detroit Airport (DTW)
to Fort Lauderdale

Flight Itinerary ✈

DATE	FROM	TO
TIME DEPARTURE	ARRIVAL	
FLIGHT NO.	ARPORT	
AIRLINE	FREQUENT FLYER	

DATE	FROM	TO
TIME DEPARTURE	ARRIVAL	
FLIGHT NO.	ARPORT	
AIRLINE	FREQUENT FLYER	

REVIEW THE DETAILS CAREFULLY WHEN BOOKING THE FLIGHT. CONSIDER ARRIVAL AT FORT LAUDERDALE. IF YOU GO THE DAY BEFORE YOUR CRUISE, YOU WILL NEED TO ALLOW TIME FOR CHECKING IN TO THE HOTEL AND OTHER THINGS. YOU MAY NOT WANT TO SLEEP LATE THAT NIGHT. YOU NEED TO ALLOW TIME TO GET OFF THE CRUISE TO GET TO THE AIRPORT ON YOUR RETURN FLIGHT. YOU MAY HAVE TO BOOK THE MAIN CABIN. YOU CAN CHOOSE YOUR SEATS WITHOUT EXTRA COST WHEN YOU CHOOSE THE MAIN CABIN OR THE MORE EXPENSIVE OPTIONS. CHECKED BAGGAGE ON DELTA AIRLINES IS $30 USD.

The Personal Item and Carryon bags are free. Be prepared to pay the extra cost. They will ask you about paying for travel insurance and to consider upgrading your ticket. It will tell you what is included in your flight. Take advantage of the free Wi-Fi while you fly. It is good to get a US or International SIM Card if you need access during the whole vacation. You won't have Wi-Fi onboard the ship except to communicate with other travelers on the ship. The airport will have wi-fi access. You will get the flight booking confirmation by email. Make sure you have this for your vacation and know when you have to be at the airport. The cruise lines have their the option to book flights through their app and website. The prices on the cruise will be higher because of the insurance and you can postpone the payment. They will hold the flight for you. If you purchase directly from the airline, you need to pay immediately to your credit card, but you can get points from the airline that you book. Flying from Toronto is more expensive. Check the baggage restrictions again a few months before your flight.

BE PREPARED TO HAVE LUNCH AFTER THE MORNING FLIGHT IF YOU FLIGHT DOESN'T INCLUDE A MEAL IF YOU ARRIVE THE AFTERNOON BEFORE YOUR CRUISE. THE AIRLINES WILL HAVE A SNACK FOR YOU ONBOARD. DECIDE IF YOU WANT TO PURCHASE AT THE AIRPORT OR EAT AT A LOCAL RESTAURANT. YOU SHOULD FAMILIARIZE YOURSELF WITH FLORIDA BEFORE YOUR ARRIVAL TO PLAN BETTER. REMEMBER, YOU MAY STILL HAVE TIME BEFORE YOUR HOTEL CHECK IN. YOU CAN EXPLORE THE AREA UNTIL THEN. TAKE OUT WHAT YOU NEED FOR THE NIGHT AND HAVE WHAT YOU NEED FOR THE CRUISE DAY EASILY ACCESSIBLE.

IF YOU WANT INTERNET DURING YOUR CRUISE FOR LESS, YOU CAN PURCHASE AN eSIM CARD FROM GIGSKY. THEY HAVE ONE FOR USA AND AMERICAS/CARIBBEAN. YOU CAN GET 7 DAYS FOR $29.99 USD. YOU NEED TO MAKE SURE YOUR PHONE IS UNLOCKED AND HAS THE eSIM OPTION. THERE ARE SOURCES ONLINE ABOUT HOW TO UPDATE YOUR PHONE'S FIRMWARE. BE CAREFUL WHEN DOING THIS AND BACKUP YOUR PHONE BEFORE YOU RESET IT. MAKE SURE YOU PUT YOUR PHONE INTO FLIGHT MODE BEFORE YOU USE THE eSIM WHEN YOU TRAVEL.

BE READY FOR TURBULENCE AND IF YOU GET EAR ACHE THEN YOU NEED TO HAVE GUM TO CHEW ON, A SNACK, AND EARPLUGS. THE EAR PLUGS MAY NOT BE ENOUGH. YOU WILL NEED TO PRETEND TO CHEW ON FOOD IF YOU DON'T HAVE ANY OF THESE. DELTA HAS THREE SEATS ON THE LEFT AND RIGHT SIDE OF THE PLANE. YOU CAN ENJOY FREE MOVIES ONBOARD THE FLIGHT, SNACK, AND BEVERAGE. IF YOU REGISTER FOR THEIR SKYMILES, YOU WILL HAVE FREE WI-FI ACCESS ON YOUR FLIGHT. YOU WILL HAVE TO CONNECT TO THEIR NETWORK ONCE THEY ARE IN FLIGHT AND SIGN INTO YOUR SKY MILES ACCOUNT. IT IS THE BEST TIME TO DO YOUR CRUISE CHECK IN IF YOU WANT IT DONE BEFORE ARRIVING AT THE HOTEL. WHEN YOU DEPART TO GO BACK TO DETROIT IF YOU TAKE THIS ROUTE, YOU WILL WANT TO CHECK IN TO YOUR FLIGHT THE NIGHT BEFORE OR THE MORNING YOU DEPART THE SHIP. IT IS IDEAL TO HAVE A US DATA PLAN SO THAT YOU CAN CHECK IN ONCE YOU ARRIVED AT FT. LAUDERDALE ON THE SECOND LAST AND LAST DAY OF YOUR CRUISE. YOU WILL BE CLOSE TO FLORIDA LATE NIGHT THE SECOND LAST DAY OF THE CRUISE.

VIA Rail

I WOULD RECOMMEND BOOKING THE TRAIN TICKET FROM TORONTO TO WINDSOR. TAKE THE TRIP AT LEAST THE DAY BEFORE THE FLIGHT. IT IS BETTER IF YOU CAN AVOID RIDING ON THE LAST TRAIN. THIS WORKS WELL IF YOU HAVE VIA RAIL POINTS. YOU NEED TO BOOK YOUR VACATION OFF AT WORK TOO.

VIA Rail Itinerary

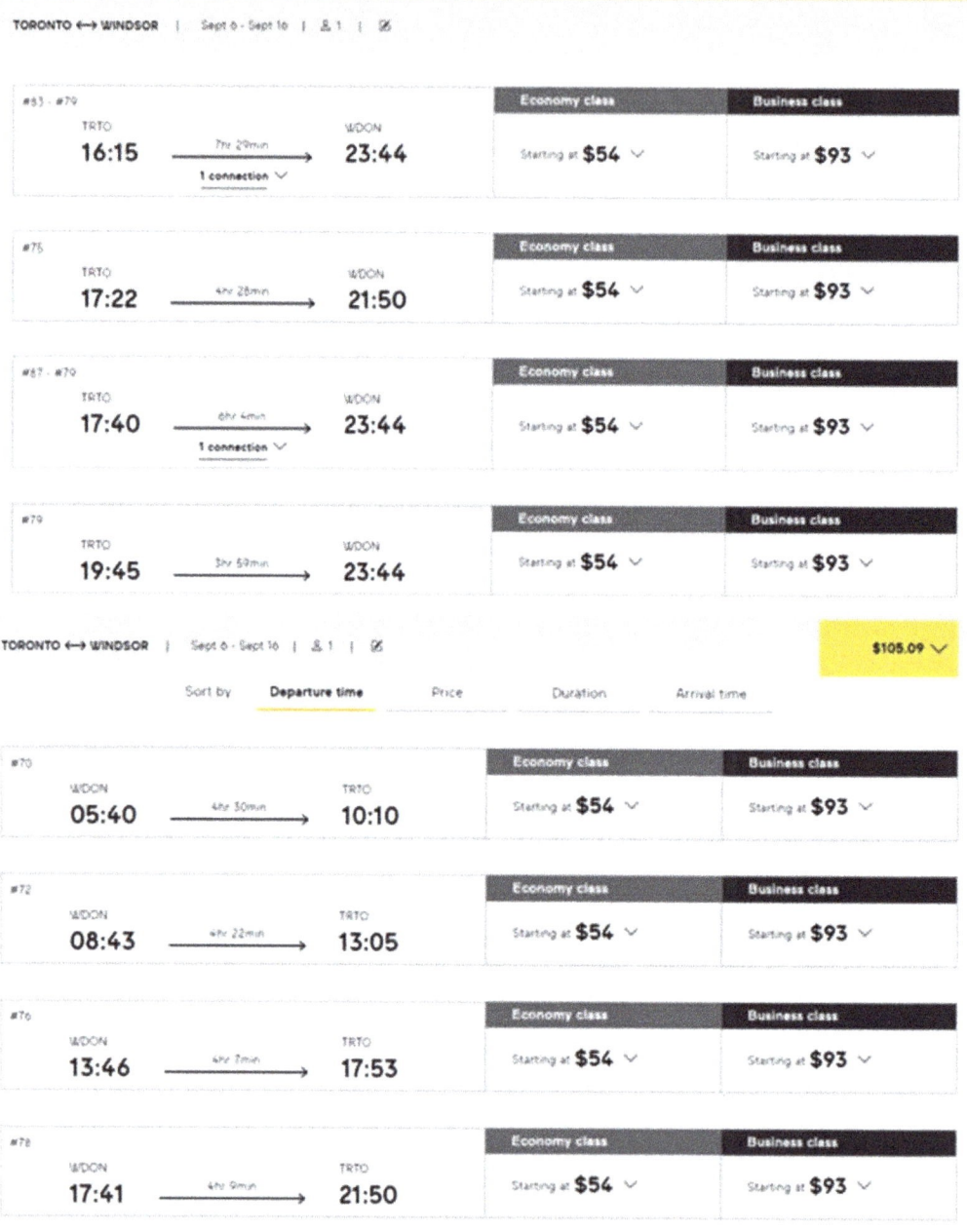

TORONTO ←→ WINDSOR | Sept 6 - Sept 16 | 🔒 1 | ✎

#63 - #79			Economy class	Business class
TRTO **16:15**	7hr 29min → 1 connection ⌄	WDON **23:44**	Starting at **$54** ⌄	Starting at **$93** ⌄

#75			Economy class	Business class
TRTO **17:22**	4hr 28min →	WDON **21:50**	Starting at **$54** ⌄	Starting at **$93** ⌄

#67 - #79			Economy class	Business class
TRTO **17:40**	6hr 4min → 1 connection ⌄	WDON **23:44**	Starting at **$54** ⌄	Starting at **$93** ⌄

#79			Economy class	Business class
TRTO **19:45**	3hr 59min →	WDON **23:44**	Starting at **$54** ⌄	Starting at **$93** ⌄

TORONTO ←→ WINDSOR | Sept 6 - Sept 16 | 🔒 1 | ✎   **$105.09** ⌄

Sort by   **Departure time**   Price   Duration   Arrival time

#70			Economy class	Business class
WDON **05:40**	4hr 30min →	TRTO **10:10**	Starting at **$54** ⌄	Starting at **$93** ⌄

#72			Economy class	Business class
WDON **08:43**	4hr 22min →	TRTO **13:05**	Starting at **$54** ⌄	Starting at **$93** ⌄

#76			Economy class	Business class
WDON **13:46**	4hr 7min →	TRTO **17:53**	Starting at **$54** ⌄	Starting at **$93** ⌄

#78			Economy class	Business class
WDON **17:41**	4hr 9min →	TRTO **21:50**	Starting at **$54** ⌄	Starting at **$93** ⌄

All fares displayed on this page are rounded, in Canadian dollars, per person and exclude all taxes. Depending on your search criteria, the fares displayed in the calendar at the top of the page may no longer be available at the time of booking. All fares are the best available at this time based on the number of tickets requested and your specified travel dates. Fares are guaranteed once you purchase your ticket.

YOU WILL RECEIVE THE VIA BOARDING PASS BY EMAIL. THEY WILL ALSO EMAIL YOU THE ITINERARY. MAKE SURE YOU HAVE THIS.

VIA Rail Itinerary

When you leave Toronto to travel to Windsor, VIA Rail will check your ticket 2-3 times. The first 1-2 times is when you are waiting in the Train station. They may check before you board the train and then when you are on the train. They will let you know when they check onboard the train. Traveling from Windsor to Toronto, they will check your train ticket when you are on the train, but you need to check which car you are supposed to board on. Your seat is assigned. If you are in business class, you get pre-boarding, meals, beverages, and snacks. The afternoon travel is the best, you can get two meals as they serve you lunch and dinner depending on the time of day you travel. There are snacks and beverages. They give you a choice of the food, but usually the best dish runs out fast. They serve alcohol and sparkling water to business class passengers. You get a better arrangement. Wi-Fi is working the same for everyone. There isn't any pre-offboarding.

COMFORT INN SUITES FORT LAUDERDALE AIRPORT AND CRUISE PORT

BOOK NOW

You can choose any hotel that is nearby. They have shuttle service from the airport to the hotel. This hotel offer free breakfast and airport shuttle. You need to request to book the shuttle to the Everglades Cruise Port. There is a charge of $15/person. If you are traveling with a group, get a quote around April 25th. Get the others to confirm to book. Avoid traffic jams. Plan to book the first shuttle leaving your hotel. Allow extra time to get to the cruise terminal. You need time for the shuttle to park and unload the luggage.

REMEMBER TO PAY A TIP TO THE DRIVER. THEY HAVE COMPLIMENTARY BREAKFAST AT THE HOTEL. THERE IS A WAFFLE MAKER FOR MAKING YOUR OWN WAFFLES. THEY HAVE THE BATTER AND OTHER THINGS YOU NEED TO MAKE IT. THE STAFF MAY HELP YOU TO MAKE IT IF YOU NEED ASSISTANCE. THEY HAVE SOME NICE JUICES IN THEIR JUICE DISPENSER AND YOUR USUAL COFFEE AND TEA. THERE ARE COMPUTERS IN THE LOBBY FOR USE IF YOU NEED TO ACCESS THE INTERNET AND DON'T USE A CELL PHONE OR HAVE A LAPTOP. THE DOUBLE QUEEN SIZE BEDROOMS ARE COMFORTABLE. THEY HAVE AN L-SHAPE COUCH WHICH WORKED NICELY FOR A FAMILY REUNION GROUP PHOTO. THERE AREN'T MUCH NEARBY STORES IN THIS AREA AND IT'S NOT CLOSE TO THE BEACH. IF YOU WANT TO EXPLORE THE AREA, YOU CAN, BUT THE WEATHER IS HOT.

BOOK YOUR TRANSPORTATION

BOOK THE SHUTTLE BUS FOR YOUR RETURN TO THE AIRPORT FROM THE CRUISE PORT ON THE LAST MORNING. FOR CANADIANS, IF YOU HAVE THE OPTION, IT IS CHEAPER TO FLY FROM THE USA TO FT. LAUDERDALE, FLORIDA. IT'S BEST TO LEAVE AN HOUR BEFORE YOU CHECK IN. YOU CAN TAKE AN UBER OR LYFT TO THE AIRPORT TOO.

IF YOU PLAN TO TAKE THE VIA RAIL TRAIN FROM TORONTO TO WINDSOR, YOU NEED TO CONSIDER THE ARRIVAL AND DEPARTURE TIME. ALLOW ENOUGH TIME TO TRAVEL TO AND FROM THE AIRPORT. YOUR OPTIONS ARE DETROIT METROPOLITAN AIRPORT OR PEARSON AIRPORT. DECIDE WHAT IS BEST FOR YOU BASED ON THE AIRLINE THAT YOU CHOOSE. IT MAY BE CHEAPER TO FLY FROM TORONTO DIRECTLY. IT IS BEST TO HAVE ENOUGH VIA RAIL TRAIN POINTS.

THEY CHARGE $10/PERSON IF YOU HAVE MORE THAN 4 PEOPLE IN A GROUP. EVERYONE IN THE GROUP SHOULD GIVE AT LEAST $1 USD TIP TO THE DRIVER. THE SAME FOR THE PORTERS AT THE CRUISE TERMINAL. EVERY TRANSPORTATION YOU TAKE, THE STAFF EXPECT TO RECEIVE A TIP. THE MINIMUM IS $1 USD. THE DRIVER WILL OFFER TO TAKE YOU ADDITIONAL PLACES IF ITS AN EXCURSION. THEY USUALLY HAVE TWO OPERATING FOR THE EXCURSIONS. YOU MAY BE VIP IF NOBODY ELSE BOOKED THE SAME EXCURSION AS YOU, BUT IT MAKES THE TRAVEL MORE ENJOYABLE.

CHECK IN TIME
JULY 25, 2024

IT'S TIME FOR YOU TO VISIT THE ROYAL CARIBBEAN APP AND TO CHECK-IN. YOU NEED TO COMPLETE ALL THE REQUIRED FORMS TODAY. THEY WILL ASK YOU FOR INFORMATION. REMIND YOURSELF ON THE CALENDAR TO DO THE CHECK IN WHEN IT OPENS. IT IS 45 DAYS BEFORE BOARDING. YOU NEED ALL YOUR PERSONAL INFORMATION. YOU NEED TO SCAN YOUR PASSPORT AND TAKE YOUR SELFIE PHOTO OF YOUR FACE, ADD YOUR CREDIT CARD INFORMATION, AND MORE. TRIPLE CHECK ALL DETAILS ARE CORRECT. THEY NEED IT FOR YOUR SEAPASS. YOU WILL NEED THE SEA PASS FROM THE PHONE APP TO CHECK IN AT THE CRUISE TERMINAL. ON THE CRUISE, YOU WILL NOT BE USING YOUR CREDIT CARD. FOLLOW ALL THE INSTRUCTIONS THAT ARE GIVEN. YOU CAN CHANGE THE CREDIT CARD ONBOARD THE SHIP. YOU WILL NEED TO DO THE HEALTH QUESTIONS THE DAY BEFORE BOARDING THE CRUISE.

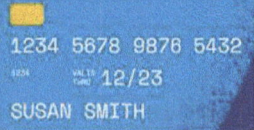

THINGS TO KNOW

You can set up a cash account at guest services instead of using your credit card. Check in is first come basis. Start earlier to get a better check in time. There are certain people that get the 11:30am check in. The next best is the 12:00pm check in. Use the app instead of the website for check in. For anyone using the website, you can also show the passport and do the selfie at the cruise terminal check in. This will lengthen the check-in process. You will do the Health Check the day for Boarding Day. It closes in 48 hours before your cruise. Details are on the app. You need your passport to check you in at the seaport on the day of the cruise. This includes those traveling with you. All details must be accurate in the document. You will need documents at the airport too. You will have a chance to select the check in time for the cruise on embarkment day. If you are new, it takes longer to check in. Become familiar with the rules and process before embarkment day. You need to watch videos about safety and

ASSIGNED A MUSTER STATION. THERE ARE THREE PARTS TO THE SAFETY. THE LAST STEP IS ON EMBARKMENT DAY BEFORE YOU BOARD THE SHIP. YOU WILL SAVE TIME DOING THE CHECK IN ON THE APP BEFORE YOUR FIRST DAY OF THE CRUISE. YOU ARE REQUIRED TO CARRY YOUR SEAPASS WHEREVER YOU GO, SO DON'T LOSE IT. YOU NEED TO CARRY CASH FOR TOO. ALLOW ENOUGH TIME TO ARRIVE AT THE TERMINAL. IT WILL DELAY YOUR CHECK IN. THEY DO SOMEBODY ELSE. DO YOUR RESEARCH OF THE CRUISE SHIP BEFORE YOUR EMBARKMENT DAY. YOU SHOULD BOOK THE SHOWS AND ACTIVITIES IN ADVANCE. THEN YOU CAN PLAN FOR THE WEEK. TAKE ADVANTAGE OF WHAT THEY HAVE TO OFFER WITHIN YOUR BUDGET. BOOK YOUR PREFERRED DINING PREFERENCES. YOU WON'T BE ABLE TO CHANGE IT. THE FLEXIBLE DINING IS THE BEST. DISCOVER THE UNIQUE ACTIVITIES. FILL OUT THE HEALTH QUESTIONNAIRE FORM BEFORE YOUR VACATION. YOU MAY GET DENIED BOARDING IF YOU DON'T OR ANSWER YES TO ANY OF THEM. ASK THE CRUISE LINE TO AVOID THE APP LOCKING YOU OUT. YOU CAN CALL THEM. IT IS RECOMMENDED TO ARRIVE EARLY AT THE TERMINAL AND THAT YOU ARRIVE AT THE CORRECT ONE TO BOARD. CHECK THE DETAILS FROM YOUR CRUISE. MAKE SURE YOU AREN'T

PACKING ANYTHING THAT THEY DON'T ALLOW ONBOARD THE SHIP. SOME ITEMS WILL BE CONFISCATED AND SET ASIDE. YOU WILL BE ABLE TO PICK UP THE CONFISCATED ITEMS AT FT. LAUDERDALE. THEY DO NOT ALLOW YOU TO HAVE THEM ONBOARD.

TRY TO GET FAMILIAR WITH THE SHIP BEFORE YOUR VACATION. MUSTER DRILL HAS A LIFE JACKET VIDEO, EMERGENCY HORN, AND MAP SHOWING THE LOCATION OF YOUR EMUSTER DRILL STATION, AND THE LAST IS TO BE COMPLETED ON THE CRUISE SHIP. IT TELLS YOU WHAT TO DO AND WHERE TO GO FOR SAFETY. MAKE SURE YOU KNOW THE DRESS CODE RULES FOR EACH RESTAURANT. YOUR OTHER OPTION IS FIXED AND YOU WILL BE EXPECTED TO EAT ON TIME. YOU MAY BE SHARING WITH OTHERS. YOU NEED TO SEE WHAT IS AVAILABLE COMPLIMENTARY. THERE ARE TOURS ON THE SHIP YOU CAN JOIN. CERTAIN RESTAURANTS ARE INCLUDED IN THE CRUISE BOOKING. JOIN THE LOYALTY PROGRAM. YOU CAN GET A BEVERAGE AREA. MAKE SURE YOU DON'T PACK THE PASSPORT IN THE LUGGAGE. YOU NEED YOUR CRUISE DOCUMENTS FOR YOU. ESSENTIALS SHOULD BE IN YOUR CARRYON LUGGAGE. YOU WILL NEED THE CARRYON LUGGAGE ON THE FIRST DAY OF THE CRUISE AND THE NIGHT BEFORE IF YOU

ARRIVE A DAY BEFORE THE CRUISE. YOU WON'T HAVE ACCESS TO THEM WHILE WAITING FOR YOUR ROOM UNTIL AFTER LUNCH. SOMETIMES THE LUGGAGE MAY NOT BE THERE WHEN YOU GET TO YOUR ROOM. MEMORIZE YOUR CABIN NUMBER (DECK AND ROOM NUMBER). STAFF REQUIRE YOU TO PAY TIPS. YOU WILL BE CHARGED THE GRATUITIES TO YOUR CREDIT CARD ATTACHED TO YOUR BOOKING RESERVATION. CALL THE SHORE EXCURSION FOR MORE DETAILS ON EXCURSIONS LIKE THE ALL DAY SNORKELING. YOU WILL NEED A LANYARD THAT HAS A PLASTIC SLEEVE FOR YOUR SEAPASS. YOU NEED TO USE BOTH SIDES. YOU WILL NEED CASH AND A CREDIT CARD FOR LOCAL STORES, RESTAURANTS, AND TIPS FOR THE STAFF. YOUR TRAVEL AGENCY WILL RECOMMEND YOU TO PRINT YOUR BOARDING PASS, BUT IT IS NOT REQUIRED. ROYAL CARIBBEAN WILL ACCESS THE ONLINE CHECK-IN DOCUMENTS AND INFORMATION THAT YOU PROVIDED PRIOR TO THE EMBARKMENT DAY AND TERMINAL CHECK IN. THEY ONLY REQUIRE THAT YOU HAVE LUGGAGE TAGS PRINTED AND ATTACHED TO YOUR LUGGAGE. THAT IS HOW THEY WILL TRACK AND DELIVERY TO YOUR CABIN. YOU STILL NEED YOUR PASSPORT ON HAND. YOU WILL NEED TO PAY OFF THE BALANCE ON YOUR ONBOARDING ACCOUNT

BEFORE YOUR LEAVE THE SHIP. THEY WILL HAVE SECURITY BRING YOU BACK IF YOU DON'T.

THE INTERNET PACKAGE VARIES PER SHIP AND FOR THIS VACATION IT WAS $19.99 USD. IT IS A COMBINATION OF SURF AND HAS THE OPTION TO WATCH MOVIES. THERE WI-FI CONNECTION IS NOT GREAT. YOU CAN SHARE THE INTERNET PACKAGE WITH OTHER USERS AND DIFFERENT DEVICES, BUT ONE PERSON CAN ONLY USE IT AT A TIME. YOU WILL NEED TO FOLLOW THE INSTRUCTIONS AND ASK DETAILS ABOUT WHETHER YOU CAN LIMIT HOW MANY DAYS YOU USE IT. THEY DON'T HAVE A CUSTOMIZED PACKAGE DEAL WHERE YOU PAY ONE PRICE FOR THE WHOLE 7 DAYS OR EVEN 30 DAYS. YOU CANNOT DO CERTAIN THINGS THAT YOU EXPECT. IT MAY BE BETTER TO GET AN ESIM CARD OR A GLOBAL SIM CARD THAT CAN BE USED FOR THE VACATION. YOU NEED TO CHECK IF YOUR PHONE CAN USE IT. YOU CAN PURCHASE 1 DAY, 7 DAYS, AND SOME MAY OFFER 30 DAYS OR MORE OF DATA, TEXT, AND CALL PLANS FOR TOURISTS.

GROUPS OF 7 OR MORE ARE SEPARATED FROM LESS FOR THE MAIN DINING ROOM. FIXED DINING WORKS BEST FOR A GROUP OF ADULTS AND SENIORS.

They rarely take long excursions. The cruise will have their own T-Shirt sales and they have T-shirts for Perfect Day CocoCay. It is best to purchase when it's on sale.

On CocoCay, it's recommended not to swim, snorkel, or scuba dive alone. Lifeguards are around and there will be other tourists swimming, but if you are not a great swimmer, it's recommended to wear a life jacket. One section is shallow, but another is deep even on the same beach. The swimming pools also have a lounge chair section in the pool. The solarium on the ship also has this.

Make sure you return the equipment back to the place you rented it from before boarding the ship when you leave Perfect Day CocoCay. They will make you sign a waiver form.

Check Airline Policies & VIA Rail Canada

- Airlines have reduced the maximum allowance for your personal item, carryon, and checked baggage.
- Measure your luggage and personal item before packing to ensure that it meets the requirements. You want to avoid paying extra for oversized.
- Airlines aren't lenient.
- If you need to take the VIA Rail to travel from Toronto to Windsor and then take the flight from Detroit, they are more concerned about the weight of the luggage. They still have maximum requirements, but are not as strict as airlines.
- Allow sufficient time to travel. You can take UpExpress to Pearson Airport if you fly to Ft. Lauderdale from Toronto.
- There are cruise vacations where you will need to fly from Toronto.
- Keep in mind that trains and flights can get delayed or Flight schedule may change.

UpExpress in Union Building to Pearson Airport in Toronto

- VIA Rail station is in the same building. Upon arrival at the VIA Rail station in Toronto. You may pass by the clock tower on the way to UpExpress. It is in the west wing.
- Purchase the ticket at the UpExpress either online or at the machines. They have three machines near the platform. The ticket is good for a year. It is in the Skywalk in Union Station in the west wing.
- Locals can use their Presto Card to pay for the UpExpress by tapping on to board and off when they disembark. They get a discounted fare.
- Seniors get a better fare.
- It is the fastest way to Pearson Airport. It takes 15 minutes to get to Terminal 3. Then you need to travel to the check in, security, and airlines gates.

Pearson Airport, Toronto

- THERE IS ANOTHER TRAIN AT THE AIRPORT THAT CONNECTS THE TERMINALS THAT YOU SHOULD TAKE.
- CHECK THE AIRPORT MAP.
- THERE IS A CIBC BANK AT THE AIRPORT.
- THEY HAVE CHECK-IN SCREENS IN MULTIPLE PLACES IN THE AIRPORT, BUT IT IS BETTER IF YOU CHECKED IN PRIOR TO FLIGHT.
- FOLLOW THE INSTRUCTIONS GIVEN BY THE AIRLINES WHEN YOU CAN CHECK-IN. IT WILL NOW ALLOW YOU TO CHECK-IN TOO EARLY OR LATE ONLINE.
- AS A LOCAL, YOU CAN TRAVEL TO UNION STATION BY BUS AND THEN SUBWAY IF YOU LIVE AWAY FROM DOWNTOWN. YOU HAVE THE OPTION OF ASKING SOMEBODY TO DROP YOU OFF AT THE AIRPORT.
- AIRPORT PARKING IS EXPENSIVE AND YOU NEED TO CALCULATE THE COST IN ADVANCE, ESPECIALLY AFTER THE PANDEMIC EVERYTHING HAS INCREASED IN PRICE.

Check Airline Policies

Packing items in the personal item which is usually a backpack

- All important documents
- Presto card (if from Toronto)
- Credit card, cash
- Laptop computer
- Car and house keys
- Medication
- Purse
- High value items: cameras, jewelry and electronic devices
- Keep liquids in standard ziploc bag as required by airlines.
- It should be 100ml total.
- Check the checked baggage is included within the requirements. Luggage that exceeds will be charged.

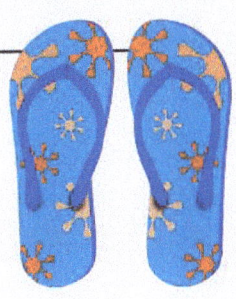

Carryon Baggage

- Luggage that exceeds will be charged.
- Avoid using bungee cords, ties, and straps to wrap your bag.
- Remove old airline tags from all bags.
- Pack all your T-shirts, shorts, hygiene related clothes, flat slippers, pajamas, swim wear and gear, less expensive items, etc in here.
- You need to make sure that your baggage is within the maximum measurement requirements. Otherwise, they will charge you.
- You should have the TSA secure lock.
- Spirit Airlines allows a higher maximum size than other airlines.

Checked Baggage

- All your formal wear, formal shoes, sandals, extra liquid products go here. There is no limit on them.
- Attach identification tags to the outside of the bags with home address and contact.
- Other items you need can go in here as long as it's TSA secure.
- Remove old airline tags from all bags.
- Check whether your checked baggage is included. Make sure it is within the maximum size. Keep items secure and safe. Do not store expensive items in this bag.
- Spirit Airlines are more generous with their baggage/luggage requirements.

Baggage Screening and Locked or Smart Bags

- TAKE THE ZIPLOC LIQUIDS BAG OUT FOR THE SECURITY CHECK.
- SHOES, WATCHES, BELT, WALLET, ETC MUST BE PLACED IN THE BIN FOR A SECURITY CHECK.
- BAGS SHOULD HAVE A TRAVEL SENTRY APPROVED OR SAFE SKIES LOCK, BUT SHOULD NOT BE LOCKED DURING BAGGAGE CHECK.
- YOU NEED TO KNOW YOUR LOCK CODES.
- THERE COULD BE DELAYS DURING THE SECURITY CHECK.
- IF YOU HAVE A SMART BAG, THE BATTERY MUST BE REMOVED, AND BATTERY SHOULD BE WITH YOU. YOU NEED TO PUT THE BATTERY INTO YOUR PERSONAL ITEM AND CARRY IN ONBOARD THE PLANE.
- KEEP LUGGAGE LOCKED.
- YOU NEED TO REMOVE ALL METALS FROM YOUR BODY FOR THE BODY SCREENING CHECK.

  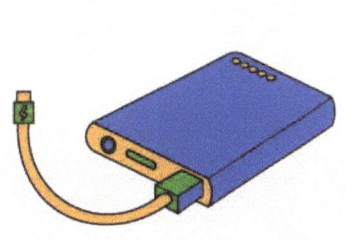 

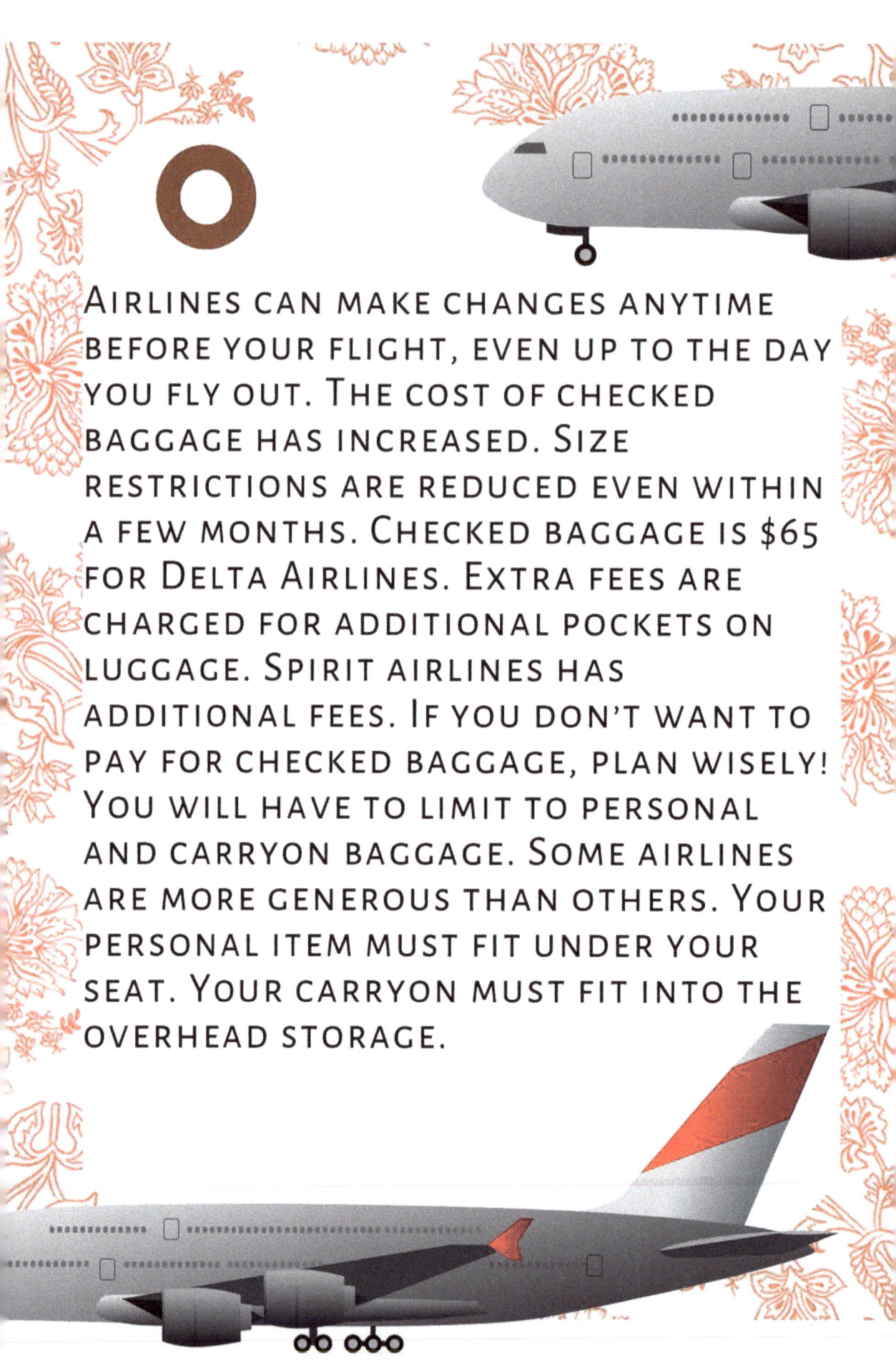

Airlines can make changes anytime before your flight, even up to the day you fly out. The cost of checked baggage has increased. Size restrictions are reduced even within a few months. Checked baggage is $65 for Delta Airlines. Extra fees are charged for additional pockets on luggage. Spirit airlines has additional fees. If you don't want to pay for checked baggage, plan wisely! You will have to limit to personal and carryon baggage. Some airlines are more generous than others. Your personal item must fit under your seat. Your carryon must fit into the overhead storage.

Reminder

- Check the details for the excursions what you need to bring to them.
- Print your shipmate ticket.
- Give yourself an hour for breakfast.
- Leave 15 minutes earlier to get to the seaport dock and line up for the excursion transportation.
- Know which line to stand at.
- Check the scheduled start time of your excursion and plan ahead.
- Set an alarm if you need help to wake up early.
- There are 2 required formal nights for the 7 nights cruise.
- Print your luggage tags in colour and tag them the night before the cruise vacation.
- You may need walkie talkies for CocoCay if you don't have the internet package.

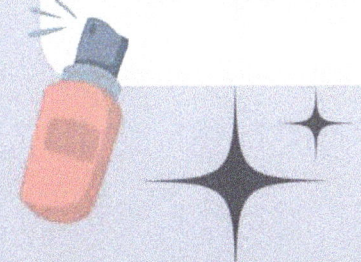

4°

Today

the weather
is partly cloudy

7 day weather forecast

Mon	Tue	Wed	Thu	Fri	Sat	Sun
4°	6°	4°	6°	5°	4°	6°

CHECK THE WEATHER BEFORE YOU TRAVEL.

Packing Checklist

Clothing

- [ ] Pajamas
- [ ] Underwear
- [ ] Bras
- [ ] Socks & Dress socks
- [ ] Tops
- [ ] Jeans/Shorts
- [ ] Dresses and Jackets
- [ ] Belt
- [ ] Swimsuits
- [ ] Workout Clothes
- [ ] Formal Outfit
- [ ] Casual Shoes
- [ ] Dress Shoes
- [ ] Sandals
- [ ] Flip Flops/Travel Slippers
- [ ] Sunglasses
- [ ] Water shoes
- [ ] Swimwear Cardigan

Miscellaneous

- [ ] Camera
- [ ] Chargers & Batteries
- [ ] Headphones
- [ ] Water bottle
- [ ] Wallet
- [ ] Phone & Charger
- [ ] Water proof cases
- [ ] Laundry detergent

Important Documents

- [ ] Passport / Visa
- [ ] Identification
- [ ] Itinerary
- [ ] Boarding Passes
- [ ] Excursion ticket, other
- [ ] Hotel Reservations
- [ ] Travel Insurance
- [ ] Emergency Contacts

Toiletries

- [ ] Shampoo
- [ ] Conditioner
- [ ] Hair Brush/Comb
- [ ] Soap
- [ ] Toothpaste
- [ ] Toothbrush
- [ ] Face Wash
- [ ] Razor
- [ ] Deodorant
- [ ] Makeup Bag
- [ ] Feminine Products
- [ ] Sunblock
- [ ] Hand & Body lotion
- [ ] Tissue paper
- [ ] Pads/Tampons
- [ ] Floss & Moutwash
- [ ] _____

How to pack your suitcase.

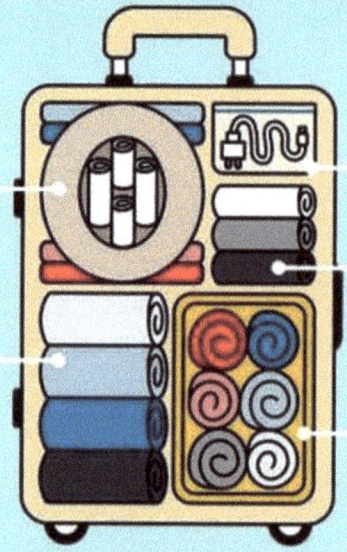

Pack hats upside down, and stuff them with soft goods

Tightly roll all casual items to maximize space

Keep charging accessories in a separate bag

Pack lighter with mix-and-match pieces in coordinating colors

Group like-items together using packing cubes

Fold bulky garments, and place them on top of rolled items

Roll socks inside shoes; place shoes in a resealable bag

Place dirty laundry in compression cubes

Opt for travel-size toiletries in a transparent bag

Use waterproof bags for wet swimwear or workout clothing

YOU SHOULD TRY TO PACK THE ITEMS AS SMALL AS POSSIBLE. PACK THIN FLAT SLIPPERS, A VISOR, AND THIN SUNGLASSES. USE BAGS WITH MULTIPLE POCKETS THAT ARE EXPANDABLE. FOLD AND ROLL AS SMALL IT AS MUCH AS POSSIBLE OR AS PACK AS FLAT AS YOU CAN.

PACKING COMPACT

If you have dress shirts, you can roll your belt inside the collar to keep the shape and pack save room. If you pack a hat, you can put foldable items inside. Roll your socks and you can pack them into the shoes. Roll your underwear in items you can hide it inside. Shoe bags are should keep your items clean. Choose neutral colours that you can mix and match. You will need a bag to carry your beach items aside from your purses. You need one formal and one casual purse. Waterproof liquids pouch is great. How about foldable travel slippers? Use travel size plastic bottles.

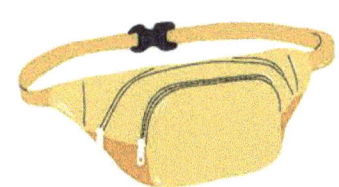

AIRPORT RULES

You will want to check TSA Rules about packing medicines and vitamins. Be aware of scammers at the airport. Take photos of your interior and exterior of your luggage. You may need it to claim compensation for any lost luggage if it happens. You will need to claim your items and check it. Items can become left behind and it may become stolen. Luggage can be left in a holding area if checked in too early. You need to line up close to a first-class agent. Airline apps are helpful to have. You can get an Air Tag to track your luggage, but it meant for iPhones, so Android phones may not work with it. You should have a durable luggage tag. Make sure you have a TSA lock and know the combination. It is not advised to bring cash when you travel. It is safer and easier to travel with digital methods, but still need some cash at the destination. Make sure that you pack sunscreen sticks, facial bars, and etc.

A THERMOS IS BETTER THAN A WATER BOTTLE. KEEP IN MIND HOW MUCH ROOM YOU HAVE. WEAR COMFORTABLE AND PROPER CLOTHES FOR YOUR FLIGHT. AVOID IT GETTING CAUGHT IN EQUIPMENT AT THE AIRPORT. YOU CAN WEAR LIGHT LEGGINGS AND SWEAT JACKETS. GET A STURDY CASE AND SCREEN PROTECTOR FOR YOUR PHONE WHEN TRAVELING. MOST PEOPLE AREN'T TRAVELING WITH A CAMERA AND RELY ON THEIR PHONE. YOU NEED TO THINK ABOUT SECURITY. NOT THAT MANY PEOPLE USE A NECK PILLOW. BACKPACK SHOULD HAVE A POCKET FOR LAPTOPS/IPADS. USE LIGHTWEIGHT LUGGAGE. FULL MEALS ARE BETTER WHEN YOU FLY THAN EATING SNACKS. KEEP ALL ELECTRONICS TOGETHER AND LIQUIDS IN THE LIQUIDS BAG IN THE FRONT POCKET OF THE PERSONAL ITEM. DISCONNECT CABLES. YOU NEED EASY ACCESS AND TO PUT THEM IN THE SECURITY CHECK BINS. KEEP ELECTRONICS NEAR YOUR WALLET, WATCH, AND PASSPORT. IT SHOULD BE THE LAST FOR THE SECURITY CHECK.

If you stay in Detroit or are taking the flight from there, hotels have shuttle service and allow you to park your car there. It is another option than parking in an airline shuttle parking lot. During rush hour, you will be waiting for at least 30 minutes for the shuttle to arrive at the airport. Traveling to your vacation destination may be smoother than your return travel. Be prepared for flight delays due to weather when flying out of Ft. Lauderdale Airport. The tunnel and bridge can have delays at the tolls. Remember to tip the driver if you are not driving.

WEEK

Day	
Mon	
Tue	
Wed	
Thurs	
Fri	
Sat	
Sun	

OUT OF OFFICE

I'm on Vacation until September 15

Chelsea Kong

DON'T FORGET TO CHANGE YOUR STATUS AT WORK AND ON YOUR PHONE SO PEOPLE KNOW YOU ARE AWAY.

Check for restaurants. Plan for dinner in Ft. Lauderdale if you arrive the day before the cruise.

Fort Lauderdale–Hollywood International Airport

Time to **Travel**

CHECK YOUR BAGGAGE AND KEEP IT WITH YOU. MAKE SURE THE LUGGAGE TAG FOR THE CRUISE IS ATTACHED BEFORE YOU CHECK IN AT THE CRUISE PORT. BE THERE 3 HOURS PRIOR TO THE FLIGHT. KEEP PASSPORT, BOARDING PASS, ETC ON HAND FOR THE SECURITY CHECK. LOOK AT YOUR GATE AND WAIT TO BE CALLED FOR BOARDING. MAKE SURE YOUR LUGGAGE TAGS ARE ON THE LUGGAGE FOR YOUR CRUISE.

SECURITY CHECK

Show your passport and boarding pass.
Pass through the screening check.
Collect your belongings.
Go to the gate to wait.
They will call by zone number.
Stay at waiting area until
You are called to board.
Have a safe flight!

Enjoy the
traveling moment

 Toronto

Florida

 Ft. Lauderdale

Brightline

TRANSPORTATION

FT. LAUDERDALE INTERNATIONAL AIRPORT HAS SHUTTLE SERVICE AVAILABLE. YOU CAN TAKE THE BRIGHTLINE TRAIN TO THE EVERGLADES SEA PORTS AT A COST. YOU SHOULD HAVE THE HOTEL SHUTTLE SERVICE BOOKED IF YOU ARE STAYING OVERNIGHT THE DAY BEFORE AND WHEN YOU RETURN IF YOU NEED AN EXTRA NIGHT'S STAY AFTER THE CRUISE. THERE ARE THE BROWARD COUNTY BUSES AND MORE. ALLOW ENOUGH TIME TO TRAVEL TO THE CRUISE TERMINAL.

FT LAUDERDALE

Sightseeing Tours
Everglades Day Safari

Check-in online helps
reduce the check-in
time at the airport.

Ticket & Transport

Affordable Hotel Rooms

5 Stars Restaurant

Explore
FT. LAUDERDALE

YOU CAN ENJOY THESE EXCURSIONS IF YOU ARRIVED A DAY EARLIER. YOU CAN ALSO EXTEND YOUR TRIP. MAKE SURE YOU BOOK IN ADVANCE.

Everglades National Park

Visit the various famous mountains with hiking trails with experienced travel guides.

Airboat Adventure

Go on fun cycling activities riding the latest models of bicycles. You can explore the famous routes while you ride too.

Holiday Lights Boat Tour

Try kayaking and get access to famous rivers and various places with experienced guides.

Remember

Bring your important belongings in the personal item. Bring your camera and have it ready. If you brought pajamas, you need to have clothes to change into and your swim wear. Once you check in at the seaport, you will need to give the porter your carryon and a checked bag. Make sure to lock them. It's better not to carry them around. The cabin is usually not ready until 2-3pm. You can explore the cruise boat, have lunch, and go swimming. They serve you the food. Be aware of what is free.

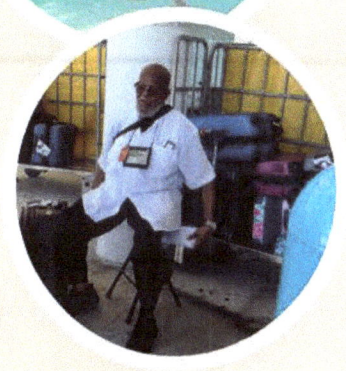

ENJOY
Social Time

Don't forget to check the shuttle details and confirm with the hotel to get to the Sea port where your cruise departs.

REMINDER

You need to tag your luggage before you leave them with the porter at the cruise terminal. Do it before you get there. The cruise line will make sure they brought your luggage to your cabin. Your cabin will not be available. This is the best time to have lunch and enjoy the adult pool. You can spend time to explore the cruise ship and take photos. Your cruise line app will be a helpful guide on board the ship.

Royal Caribbean has deck plans, itinerary, your room, and more. It is the only communication that you have on the cruise that is free. Book the cruise shows you want to watch in advance. Your Sea Pass will be your most important card on the vacation.

Check the beverages, food items, and services included in your cruise booking. They charge for everything not included. There is a water filter onboard. Some beverages are free.

CRUISE TERMINAL CHECK IN

Make sure that you have your essential items in the carryon luggage and your electronics and passport in your personal item. You should double check the time scheduled for your cruise terminal check in. Be prepared to catch your ride to the cruise terminal. You can also sit if you arrive there early. Make sure you do not pack your passport in your luggage. You won't be able to get access to it. You need to know which line to stand at for check in. They will give you details on the emuster drill station before you get to the terminal. You need to check the app. You will need to know what room you booked and cruise deck to check in. You will have time to enjoy the ship. You have a few options for complimentary food at Windjammer marketplace, Sorrento's Pizza, the Main Dining. and El Loco Fresh. There are lounges you can check out too.

FT. LAUDERDALE EVERGLADES CRUISE PORT

- Take the transit to the Ft. Lauderdale Seaport to arrive by 11AM at the earliest.
- Check-in is 11:30AM–1PM.
- Have your booking confirmation and passport ready.
- Access Wi-Fi
- They will give you the tickets, keys, SeaPass for all the seaports, etc.
- You need the SeaPass and tickets for the excursions.

CRUISE TERMINAL
ON EMBARKMENT DAY

Embarkment Day

You will need to check in at the cruise terminal. You need to go through the screening process and show your passport. The cruise line has lineups and you need to know which one to go to. They separate new members from those who have been on multiple cruises. You get perks if you have been on several cruises already. You can check the different types of membership that they have online. You will have a porter to check in on the first day. The porter will take your luggage and the service is free. They will bring it to the ship. You need to show the passport multiple times at the terminal. You need to know which line to go to for your stateroom. Those who bought the key package need to look for that line. Everyone else has a standard line. You need to show your pass and ID to show in additional line up. Security screening is shorter than at the airport. They expect $2-3 tip for taking your checked baggage. You need to decide if you want to give them the carryon, but make sure you keep the passport, paperwork, cellphone etc in your personal baggage. Security will check your

LUGGAGE. GROUPS CAN CHECK IN TOGETHER, BUT LUGGAGE IS DELIVERED SEPARATELY. YOU SHOULD EXPLORE THE SHIP ON THE FIRST DAY TO FIND THE BEST VIEWS AND WHERE TO GO FOR THE SHOWS, FOOD, ACTIVITIES, ETC. THERE ARE SEATS FOR YOU WHILE YOU WAIT. YOU WILL WALK TO THE SHIP AFTER THE CHECK IN. YOU WILL NEED TO DO THE eMUSTER DRILL BEFORE YOU DO ANYTHING ELSE. ENJOY THE WINDOW VIEW FROM YOUR ROOM THAT OVERLOOKS THE PROMENADE, BUT BE AWARE THAT PEOPLE CAN SEE YOU. USE THE CURTAINS WHEN YOU WANT PRIVACY. YOU CAN ALSO WATCH SOME SHOWS WITHOUT LEAVING YOUR STATEROOM. IT IS QUIET SO YOU CAN SLEEP. YOUR INTERIOR STATEMENT HAS A NOTE ON THE BACK OF THE DOOR THAT SAYS LUGGAGE AT 3:00PM. MAKE SURE YOU CHECK THE APP FOR THE SCHEDULED TIME TO DO THE GUEST SAFETY BRIEFING. ROYAL CARIBBEAN HAS IT SCHEDULED IN MY CALENDAR FOR 10:15AM (5 HOURS 30 MINUTES). IF YOU CLICK ON IT, IT WILL GIVE YOU THE DECK AND DINING ROOM NUMBER. FOR THIS VACATION, IT SAID DECK 4 AND D23. THE SAFETY VIDEOS AND TIPS PLUS THE MEDICAL FACILITY ON DECK 1 IS PROVIDED FOR DAY 1. THERE ARE SAFETY DETAILS FOR CHILDREN TOO. YOU CAN COMPLETE THE ONBOARD EMERGENCY CHECK IN LATER ON AFTER LUNCH. MOST PEOPLE GO TO WINDJAMMER ON DECK 11 TO EAT LUNCH AFTER THEY BOARD. STATEROOMS ARE NOT ACCESSIBLE.

If you visit your stateroom deck before it's ready, you will find no access. The hallway doors are closed. When they are ready, you can walk through the hallways to the room. You will find your SeaPass Card in a small pocket envelope waiting for you. Inside your room. With two people sharing the room, both SeaPass Cards will be inside. They have information that you need to know about the cruise, but if you want the daily planner printed, you need to go to Guest Services to get one every day. They give you the excursion tickets inside an envelope that shows your name on it. Keep in mind there are two people that usually stay in a stateroom. It is required that you wash your hands before eating meals. They do have Room Service but check if there is an additional cost. They will charge your account. You need to tip the Room Service Staff too. You should check with Guest Services to see what charges are on your statement. If you do any cancellations, it is reflected on the account as a credit. Then it goes to the credit card. The Onboard credit will show as a non-refundable balance.

ON BOARD THE CRUISE

1ST TO 10TH DECK
ARE STATEROOMS.
THIS SHIP HAS 15 DECKS.

Keep watch

You might see the planes taking off when you go to the restaurant or buffet. It's wise to have your camera with you just in case and be ready to take videos and photos. It's rare to see them.

Explore food and more

Explore your options on board the cruise. You can eat at the restaurant. Starbucks is not included in your cruise booking. Keep in mind the extra food, snacks, beverages, gifts, lessons, activities, services etc are charged to your Seapass and your credit card on the last night of the cruise. The website tells you what services are available. You can also book additional ones by visiting the service desk onboard the cruise boat. It may cost you more. On formal nights, they will serve lobster and seafood dishes. Because of the pandemic, they reduced the food options so there are fewer shrimp and no big scallops. You might get Linguini served with pearl scallops. You can ask for another serving. The Buffet is always open, but the restaurants are not. You can get additional food items at the buffet to eat if you still need more food, fruits, and drink.

IMPORTANT
ANNOUNCEMENT

Sanitize and wash hands regularly. The water in your stateroom/cabin is not in your booking. You are charged to your room. Keep this in mind and let the person sharing with you know. They may charge both of you. You will notice it on the bill in addition to the gratuities.

Allow yourself half an hour for breakfast and 15 minutes to be at the Sea Port for your excursion ride. Follow the instructions on your ticket. You will have time to eat a late lunch when you return. Your dinner is based on the time you reserved your table.

Interior Room

CHECK YOUR ROOM THAT YOU HAVE EVERYTHING YOU NEED AND KNOW WHAT IS AVAILABLE.

Freedom of the Seas

LUNCH AT WINDJAMMER

Freedom of the Seas

ROYAL PROMENADE

Happy birthday!

Chelsea

HAPPY

BIRTHDAY

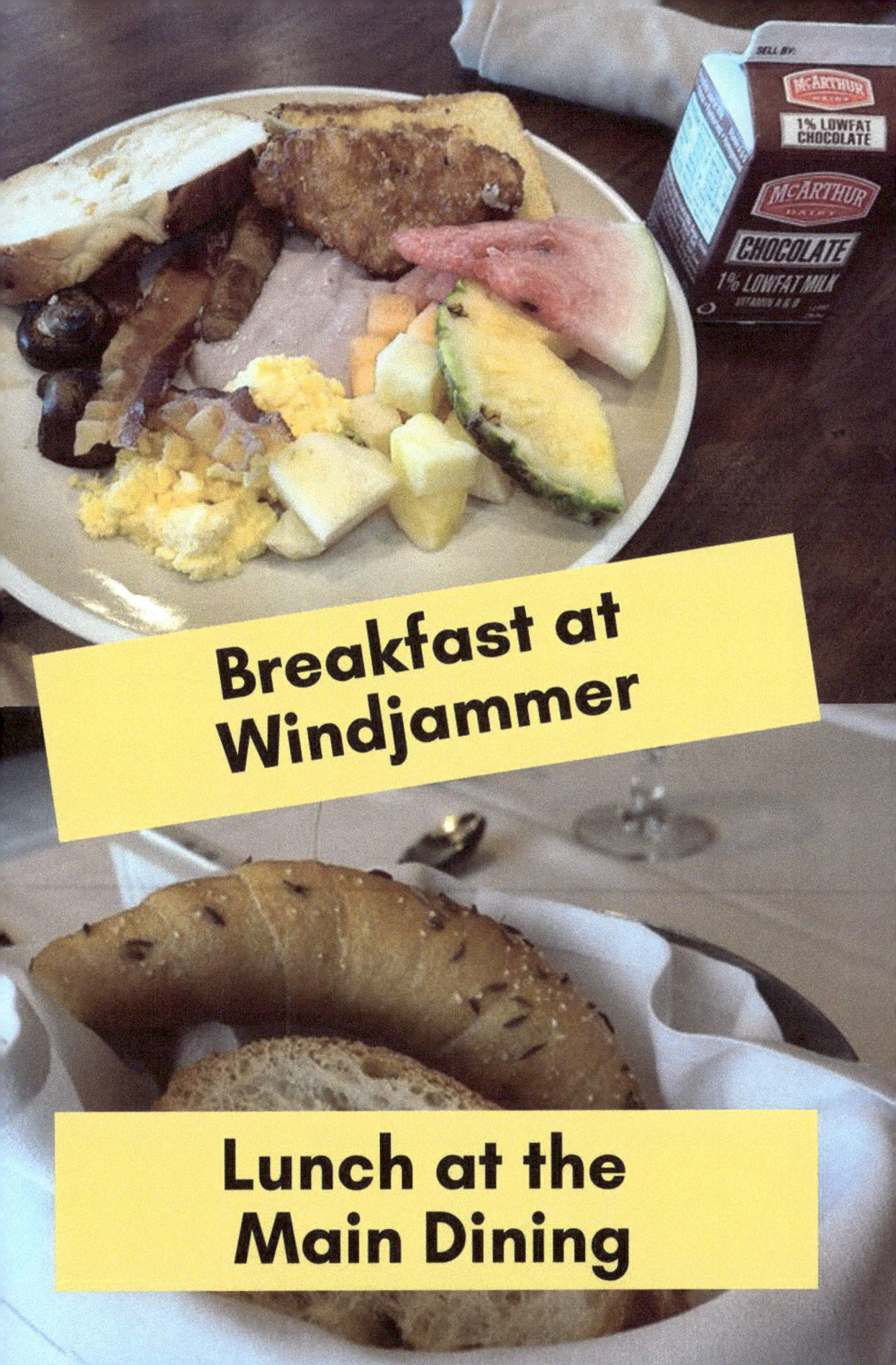

Breakfast at Windjammer

Lunch at the Main Dining

Lunch at the
Main Dining

Formal Night

Freedom on Ice

DINNER

Explore George Town, Grand Cayman

Stingray city is a great snorkel location for stingrays. You can enjoy the sun as you take a walk on Seven Mile Beach. Take a tour to swim with turtles and dolphins, kite surfing, kayak, paddle boarding sailing, and more. You can get photos taken for you at a cost.

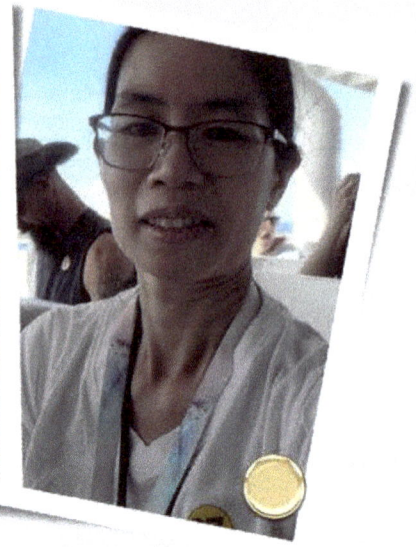

Royal Caribbean had us go to the Royal theatre to wait to be called. Each excursion has a team number. When they are ready, they tell us to go out to the mini boat. This takes us to Grand Cayman Port. Then we have to line up under our assigned tent and go take a bus to a boat. The boat will take us to Stingray City and Starfish Point Beach. You can ask a tourist to help you take photos or you can have the excursion host take them for you and they will charge you a fee. You can get them emailed or Air Dropped to your phone. He can send by WhatsApp. The captain that I had is 22 years old and operates with family. He tells everyone to take off their shoes.

MAKE SURE YOU USE WATERPROOF OR WATER RESISTANT SUNSCREEN OR SUNBLOCK. THE SUN IS VERY STRONG AND WILL BURN YOUR SKIN. IT WILL YOUR PALE OR FAIR SKIN TURN BROWN. YOU WILL NEED TO USE ALOE VERA IF YOU GET A SUNBURN AND BODY LOTION, IDEALLY WITH VITAMINS OR MINERALS. COLD COMPRESSES, COLD SHOWERS. YOUR SKIN WILL FEEL ITCHY IF YOU DON'T HAVE BODY LOTION ON IT. IT GOT DRIED BY THE SUN. BE PREPARED FOR DELAYS GOING AND RETURNING FROM THE EXCURSION. FOR GRAND CAYMAN, THEIR MONEY IS WORTH MORE THAN THE USD. THE BENEFIT IS THERE ARE NO ADDITIONAL FEES WHEN YOU PURCHASE FROM THE LOCAL SHOPS AT THE DIFFERENT PORTS. IT'S GOOD TO TRY LOCAL FOODS AND GET SOUVENIRS IF ITS YOUR FIRST TIME.

WELCOME
TO THE
CAYMAN ISLANDS

Tourists that decide not to take an excursion, can still enjoy Grand Cayman. You take a walk to explore the local shops near the cruise port. Remember to take your passport with you or other Photo ID. They will check and after that there is a check point for your sea pass before you can take the mini boat back to the cruise ship. You have enough time to explore on shore what they have in the area if you aren't doing any excursions. If you find a Starbucks, they will have WiFi available that you can connect to. Most of the time you won't have free WiFi. Lunch is not provided for the short excursions. There is more than one stingray and Starfish excursion offered by this cruise line. The other one is a few hours longer. It includes a stopover to get lunch. Some have lunch included, but it can be 6 hours. This is in general for any excursion offered by this cruise line. There are places designed so you can take photos too.

Stingray City

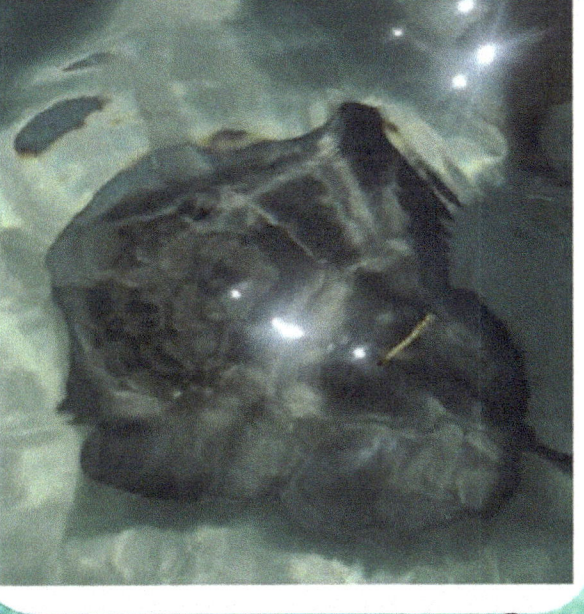

This is my happy place
Fun with the stingray!

Starfish
Point Beach

There is also a semi-formal night where you dress up for dinner at the main dining. You still need to dress up if you are going to eat dinner at the Windjammer as it is required for everyone to dress based on what night it is. Formal nights are usually during sea days. There is at least one night where the lobster tail is complimentary in the menu. Otherwise, you need to pay $16.99 USD, but the waiter will tell you there is 20% discount. The discount is offered for other nights when lobster tail is offered, but not complimentary. The waiter will also offer to remove the lobster tail meat for you to eat. There are also late night events that you can join if you can stay up late. They start breakfast quite early in the morning when its departure day. It can be open as early as 7am. The waiter will tell you what theme night it is during every dinner that you eat at the main dining. You may notice certain soups or appetizers are repeated in your cruise.

Dinner

MATCHA CREAM PUFF AT
CAFE PROMENADE

BREAKFAST & LUNCH

ENJOY THE FALLS
FALMOUTH, JAMAICA

Try the Dune Buggy, Blue Hole and River Tubing, and Bamboo Rafting. Consider taking an excursion to Ocho Rios and visit the famous Dunn's River Falls. It's an iconic site. Check out Burwood Beach. Try their rum, rum cake and blue mountain coffee. You can buy them there to take home too. Just ask the Tour Guide for your excursion to bring you there.

Montego Bay

If you are just visiting the cruise port, you can ask the information booth. Any alcohol and blue mountain coffee you buy, you need to talk to the crew staff. They will hold onto it and return them to you. They will put a label on it and make sure it goes to your stateroom. You will be able to pack it in the checked baggage. You will need to ask the staff if your luggage does it detained or any items are missing. Luggage or items can be delayed in being delivered to your stateroom. You need to claim it at the border when you return. Konoko Falls and Dunn's Falls are not recommended for people with health conditions. Small children should not climb the falls. You must wear water shoes for this excursion, waterproof case for your phone, and should have a swim suit or trunks as you will get wet. It is best to leave the other belongings including the towel in the shuttle. They put a wrist band on you at the start of the visit. You should take a restroom break before you

CLIMB THE FALLS. YOU CAN'T STOP MID WAY AND GO BACK. YOU WILL HAVE TO CLIMB TO THE TOP. THE GUIDE WILL ASK YOU WHEN YOU ARE READY TO PROCEED. THEY WILL MAKE SURE YOU MAKE IT BACK SAFELY. THEY WILL LEAVE YOU ONCE YOU REACHED THE LAST PART OF THE VISIT. YOU WILL BE DIRECTED TWO OPTIONS OF CHOICE. YOUR DRIVER IS OPEN TO GIVE YOU TIME TO LOOK AROUND LONGER OR TAKE YOU TO GET SOMETHING TO EAT. THAT IS THE BEST TIME TO PURCHASE THE RUM AND COFFEE AT A LOCAL SHOP BEFORE RETURNING TO THE SHIP. HE WILL SHARE ABOUT DIFFERENT PLACES ON THE DRIVE GOING TO KONOKO FALLS. IF YOU ARE VIP WITH NOBODY ELSE JOINING YOU, YOU HAVE MORE BENEFIT. YOU WILL ALSO GET A RIDE BACK TO THE CRUISE PORT LOCAL SHOPS AND BUSINESSES. YOU CAN EXPLORE THERE OR COME BACK AFTER LUNCH. JAMAICANS ONLY COME OUT EARLY MORNING OR LATE AFTERNOON TO THE BEACH. SOME SHOPS MAY NOT BE OPEN UNTIL THE LATE AFTERNOON. LOCALS HAVE SALES OFTEN TO ATTRACT TOURISTS. THE RUM DEALER GAVE A DISCOUNT AT THIS ONE LOCAL SHOP AND THEY MAY GIVE FREE MUGS TOO.

KONOKO FALLS

KONOKO FALLS

MAHOE TREE

FLORAL AND MORE

A TOUR GUIDE SHARES INFORMATION ABOUT THE FLORAL, TREES, AND MORE. THEN YOU WILL BE TOLD TO GO DOWN A SET OF WOODEN STAIRS TO THE BOTTOM TO MEET ANOTHER GUIDE WHO WILL LEAD YOU TO WALK UP THE WATERFALL. IT'S A LONG WAY DOWN THE SEVERAL STAIRCASES. THEY HAVE A SPRING WATER FACET HERE. THE FALLS ARE BEAUTIFUL. THERE IS A POOL AT THE BOTTOM. THE CLIMB IS LONG TOO.

Botannical Garden

Zoo

Zoo

A fun place for family!

KONOKO FALLS

Shipmate

IN THE AFTERNOON, THERE WAS A PARADE WITH SINGING AND DANCING. THEY HAVE DIFFERENT SHOWS AT NIGHT. THE CRUISE DIRECTOR TELLS YOU WHAT SHOWS ARE AVAILABLE AT THE FIRST SHOW.

Breakfast

PICKLEBALL

Take time to have some fun and play! Beginners and pros can enjoy this. If you haven't tried this game, you will find it is easy to learn and fun to play. It is easier than table tennis. Children will also want to play. You need to book it in advance. It is a popular game.

PICKLEBALL FREE PLAY TIME IS USUALLY FROM 9-11AM. YOU CAN PLAY THE FIRST ROUND WITHOUT SIGNING UP IF NOBODY IS ON THE COURT, BUT AFTER THAT YOU NEED TO SIGN UP. YOU MAY JOIN WITH OTHER TRAVELERS ONBOARD, ESPECIALLY IF YOU PLAY AS A FAMILY, BUT EVEN COUPLES MAY GET SEPARATED. IT IS FIRST COME FIRST SERVE. YOU CAN FIND THE SPORTS DECK ON DECK 12 OF THE SHIP. THE FREEDOM DUNES IS THE MINI GOLF FOUND ON DECK 13. DECK 14 HAS THE STAR LOUNGE. IF YOU VISIT DECK 15, YOU WILL FIND THE HELIPAD THERE FOR EMERGENCIES. IF THE SHIP IS NEAR THE SHORE, THEY WILL SEND IT BACK TO PORT TO HAVE THE PERSON TRANSPORTED TO THE HOSPITAL. OTHERWISE, THEY WILL HAVE A HELICOPTER FLY IN AND AIR LIFT THE PERSON TO THE HOSPITAL. THEY HAVE PAID LESSONS DURING BEFORE THE FREE-TIME AND OTHER ACTIVITIES AFTER IT. THEY MAY HAVE OTHER TIMES SCHEDULED FOR PAID LESSONS. YOU WILL ALSO FIND TABLE TENNIS/PING-PONG

TABLES, HACKY SACKS FOR TOSSING, THE WATER PARK SLIDER, FLOWER RIDER, AND JOHNNY ROCKET'S RESTAURANT ON THIS DECK. YOU CAN ALSO GET A PLEASANT VIEW OF THE SPLASHAWAY BAY AND OTHER POOLS. THEY HAVE LOUNGE CHAIRS AND BENCHES TO SIT ON. THERE ARE ALSO TWO WASHROOMS AVAILABLE FOR USE. WHEN IT GETS WINDY, IT BECOMES A CHALLENGE TO PLAY SPORTS. IT IS A LOT OF FUN. THERE WAS ONE TIME IT RAINED WHEN IT WAS A NICE DAY FOR PLAYING MINI GOLF. ON SEA DAYS/CRUISING DAYS, YOU WILL WANT TO PLAY SPORTS ON THE SHIP. YOU CAN ALSO PLAY INDOORS. THEY HAVE A SECTION CALLED PLAYMAKERS. YOU CAN GO THERE. THEY ALSO HAVE SOME MUSIC AND OTHER THINGS. YOU CAN ALSO CUT THROUGH HERE TO GET TO THE ROYAL THEATRE, BUT YOU NEED TO TAKE THE STAIRS TO GO DOWN ONE LEVEL. THE FRONT AND BACK OF THE SHIP ARE NOT CONNECTED ON CERTAIN FLOORS.

ON THE FREEDOM OF THE SEAS, YOUR MOST IMPORTANT FLOORS ARE DECKS 1, 3

4, 5, 11, 12, AND 13. THE OTHER IS YOUR STATEROOM FLOOR. DECK 11 HAS WINDJAMMER BUFFET, SPLASHAWAY BAY, THE POOLS, LOUNGE SEATS, COUCHES, SOME FOOD, HOT TUB, TOWEL SERVICE, AND SPRINKLES. DECK 1 IS THE GANGWAY WHICH YOU NEED TO EXIT THE SHIP TO VISIT THE CRUISE PORTS. DECK 5 IS GUEST SERVICES, ROYAL PROMENADE WITH CAFE PROMENADE, SOLENTRO'S PIZZA, SHOPS, AND MORE. THERE ARE STAIRS THAT GO TO PLAYMAKERS AND ALSO STAIRS THAT TAKE YOU TO DOWN TO STUDIO B. ROYAL THEATRE IS AT THE FRONT OF THE SHIP AND NOT DIRECTLY CONNECTED TO THE REST OF THE DECK ON THAT LEVEL. I THINK IT IS ON DECK 4. DECK 4 AND 3 IS ALSO THE MAIN DINING WHERE YOU CAN HAVE BREAKFAST, LUNCH AND DINNER, BUT THEY ONLY SERVE ALL THREE MEALS DURING SEA DAYS. ON PORT DAYS, THEY ONLY SERVE BREAKFAST AND DINNER. YOU NEED TO GO TO THE BUFFET FOR LUNCH. WINDJAMMER IS AVAILABLE FOR ALL THREE MEALS, BUT CLOSES USUALLY 9PM. CERTAIN DAYS THEY CLOSE A BIT LATER. CHECK THE ROYAL CARIBBEAN

APP FOR MORE DETAILS ABOUT RESTAURANTS OPTIONS. THEY CHANGE THE MENU EVERY NIGHT FOR DINNER IN THE MAIN DINING, BUT NOT FOR BREAKFAST. EVERY NIGHT IS A DIFFERENT THEME. THE APP WILL TELL YOU WHICH DAY IS FORMAL NIGHT AND WHAT THEY WANT YOU TO WEAR. THE WAIT STAFF AND RESTAURANT STAFF ARE FRIENDLY. THEY HAVE SECURITY TO DECIDE WHICH TABLE IS VACANT THAT YOU CAN SIT AT DURING BREAKFAST TIME. DINNER TIME TABLES ARE RESERVED, SO THEY DIRECT YOU TO THE TABLE ASSIGNED TO YOUR SEAPASS. YOUR SEAPASS ALSO TELLS YOU YOUR STATEROOM. YOU CAN HAVE AN EXTRA ROOM KEY MADE, BUT IT WILL NOT HAVE THE OTHER DETAILS ON IT. YOU WILL ALWAYS NEED TO SCAN YOUR SEAPASS WHENEVER YOU BOARD AND LEAVE THE SHIP. USE A LANYARD IS IDEAL, BUT YOU WILL NEED TO REMOVE THE CARD OUT WHEN YOU ACCESS THE ROOM. ROOM ATTENDANTS TEND TO BE HELPFUL. EVERY SO MANY DAYS, THEY WILL LEAVE YOU A DIFFERENT TOWEL ANIMAL IN YOUR ROOM. MAIN DINING

ALSO ALLOWS YOU TO HAVE MULTIPLE APPETIZERS AND MAIN DISH YOU LIKE TO ORDER AGAIN AFTER YOU HAVE HAD YOUR FIRST APPETIZER AND MEAL. JUST KEEP IN MIND THAT IF YOU ARE IN THE FIXED TIME, YOU NEED TO FINISH ON TIME. YOU CAN TAKE YOUR DESSERT TO EAT IN YOUR STATEROOM EVEN YOUR BIRTHDAY CAKE. THEY WILL GIVE YOU A COVER FOR THE PLATE IF YOU ASK. THEY HAVE A NICE TEAM OF CHEFS PREPARING THE FOOD. TWICE DURING THE CRUISE, THEY INTRODUCED THEIR TEAM AND RECOMMENDED GIVING AN APPLAUSE TO THEM. THE WATERS GAVE A SONG AND DANCED ON THE SECOND LAST NIGHT OF THE CRUISE. THEY WERE CIRCLING AROUND DECK 3. THAT IS THE MAIN LEVEL. WINDJAMMER STAFF WILL REMIND YOU EVERY TIME TO WASH YOUR HANDS BEFORE EATING AND THEY EVEN HAVE SOMEBODY SINGING IT AS A SONG AND PLAYING THE GUITAR. YOU WILL MEET FAMILIES TRAVELING EVEN IN SEPTEMBER WITH CHILDREN AND THOSE WITH OLDER CHILDREN. THEY HAVE POOL PARTIES AND MOVIES PLAYING AT THE POOL.

Dinner

Studio B - Freedom on Ice

Mario and Daniel Comedy Show

Freedom on ice in Studio B was having its last contract of shows during this cruise. They had 10-year contract arrangement. It's a group of young adult professionals that skate on ice to music, so there is dancing involved. They have a mix of themes and it's well performed. Studio B is the Ice Rink. In the Royal Theatre, you will always have shows every night. They usually run from 7-8pm or at 8pm. There is a second show at 9pm and there may be late shows at 11pm. The cruise director will announce the shows, but it is also in the app and on the daily calendars/bulletins. Royal Theatre has the production show, comedy, famous singers, and more. The last night of this cruise they had Elisa Furr who sings tribute to Celine Dion. If a singer can't make it to the original schedule, they will fill in with their production team. They are also professional singers and dancers. The music band are professionals. Elisa Furr also

ANNOUNCED THAT SHE WOULD JOIN AS A MEMBER ON THE CRUISE AFTER SHE FINISHED HER PERFORMANCE. SHE WAS THE SPECIAL GUEST THAT THEY WANTED TO BRING ONBOARD EARLIER IN THE WEEK. SHE COULDN'T MAKE IT ON THE SCHEDULED DAY, BUT SHE COULD ON THE SECOND LAST DAY OF THE CRUISE. THEY ALSO ANNOUNCE WHEN THERE IS A TIME ZONE CHANGE AND REMIND YOU TO SET YOUR CLOCK BACK ONE HOUR ON THE PHONE AND HOW IT SHOULD BE DONE. THEY WILL REMIND YOU WHEN TO CHANGE IT BACK ONE HOUR AHEAD. THEY TELL YOU AT THE BEGINNING OF EVERY SHOW NOT TO USE FLASH PHOTOGRAPHY. YOU CAN STILL TAKE PHOTOS WITH YOU PHONE. YOU NEED TO MAKE SURE THE NIGHT SETTINGS ARE ON AS THE LIGHTING AFFECTS THE QUALITY EVEN WHEN USING A PROFESSIONAL CAMERA IF ITS NOT SET RIGHT IT WILL NOT CAPTURE WELL. IT HAPPENED DURING THIS CRUISE. YOU DON'T NOTICE WHEN YOU ARE FOCUSED ON WATCHING THE SHOW. YOU CAN GET ICE CREAM AT SPRINKLES UP TO A CERTAIN TIME IN THE EVENING.

It's time for
NASSAU, BAHAMAS

Nassau Walking Tour

TOUR QUEEN'S STAIRCASE MADE OF LIMESTONE AND IT IS STEEP TO CLIMB. VISIT FORT FINCASTLE, RAWSON PARLIAMENT SQUARE, AND QUEEN VICTORIA'S STATUE.

Discover Nassau Harbor Cruise

ENJOY BEAUTIFUL CRYSTAL-BLUE WATERS IN PARADISE ISLAND HARBOR ON A CATMARAN. TAKE A VISIT TO SEE THE EXCELLENT VIEWS OF ATLANTIS, HISTORIC LANDMARKS, AND CELEBRITY HOMES.

Nassau by Land and Sea

TOUR THE 18TH-CENTURY FORT FINCASTLE, QUEEN'S STAIRCASE, AND MORE. A FANTASTIC VIEW AND ENJOY COMPLIMENTARY FRUIT PUNCH.

Check out Baha Bay Water Park at Baha Mar, Atlantis Dolphin Cay Playtime, Blue Lagoon Island for a shark encounter, Atlantis Resort for the largest water park in the Caribbean on Paradise Island. There are water trampolines, kayaks, and stand-up paddleboards. You can do your own walking tour. Stay in a group. Be careful of a man who tells you history wants a tip. You can get a rum cake. It's delicious and try their blue mountain coffee.

Nassau, Bahamas

ENJOYING NASSAU, BAHAMAS

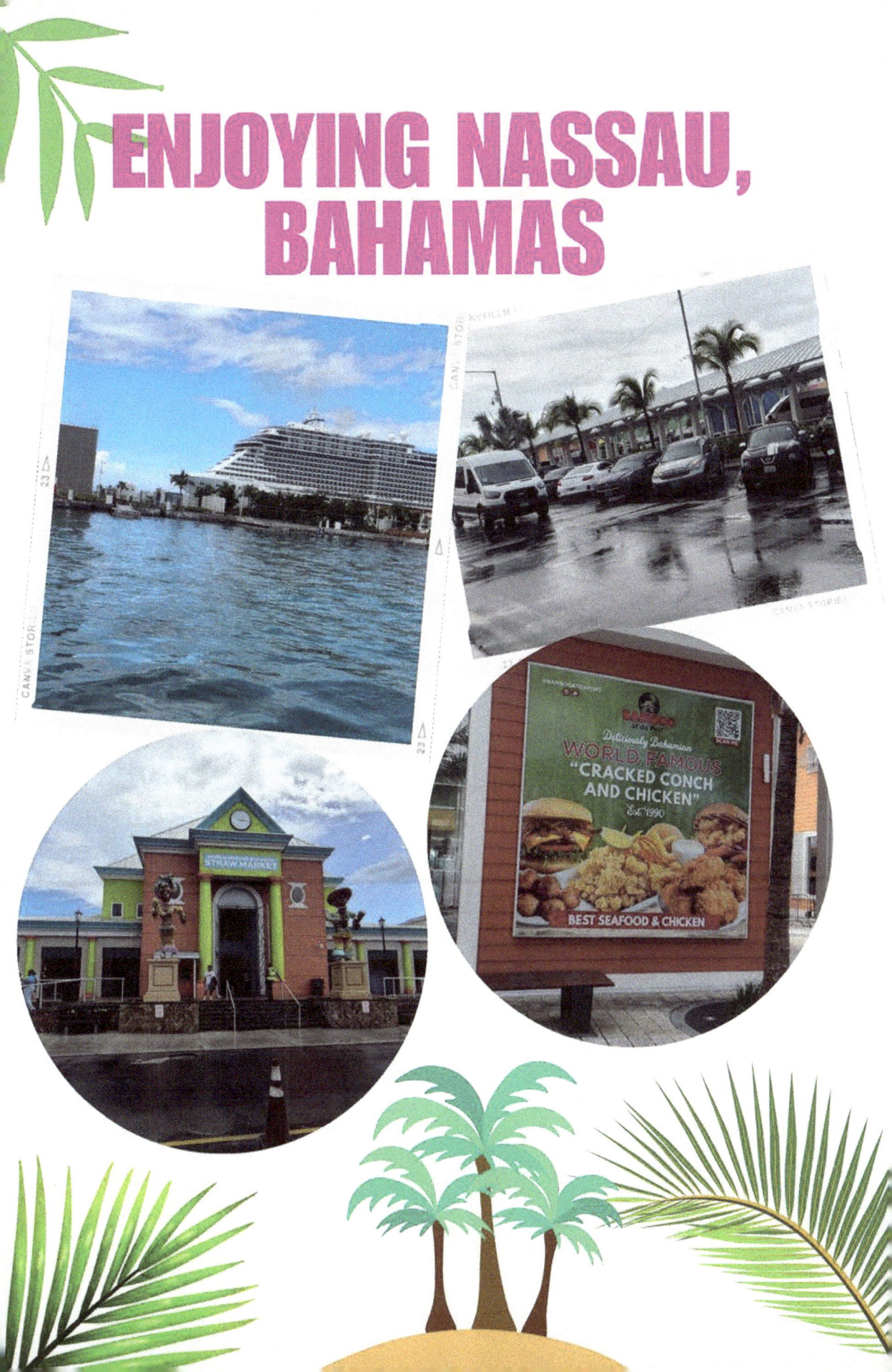

CRUISEPORT
VISIT

Nassau

MY
Lunch

Dinner

BREAKFAST

Cococay, Bahamas

STEP OUTSIDE YOUR COMFORT ZONE, TAKE THE PATH LESS TRAVELED, AND DISCOVER THE WONDERS THAT AWAIT. GET READY FOR AN EXHILARATING JOURNEY OF SELF-DISCOVERY AND UNFORGETTABLE EXPERIENCES. MOST OF THE FOOD IS FREE. THE TRAM SERVICE, POOLSIDE AND BEACHSIDE LOUNGERS, UMBRELLAS, FRESHWATER SHOWERS, CHANGING ROOMS, AND RESTAURANTS ARE COMPLIMENTARY. YOU CAN WALK FROM ARRIVAL PLAZA TO MOST OF THE COMPLIMENTARY OPTIONS.

ISLAND

BEACHES

THRILL PARK

Perfect Day at CocoCay, Bahamas

PRIVATE ISLAND FUN!

HIDEAWAY BEACH, COCO BEACH CLUB, OASIS LAGOON, CHILL ISLAND, THRILL WATERPARK. CHECK THE ISLAND MAP AHEAD OF TIME. PLAN THE PLACES THAT YOU WANT TO GO TO SAVE TIME AND MONEY. THERE ARE PLACES THAT ARE CHEAP AND OTHERS COST MORE. ASK FOR TIPS. YOU SHOULD HAVE BREAKFAST FIRST.

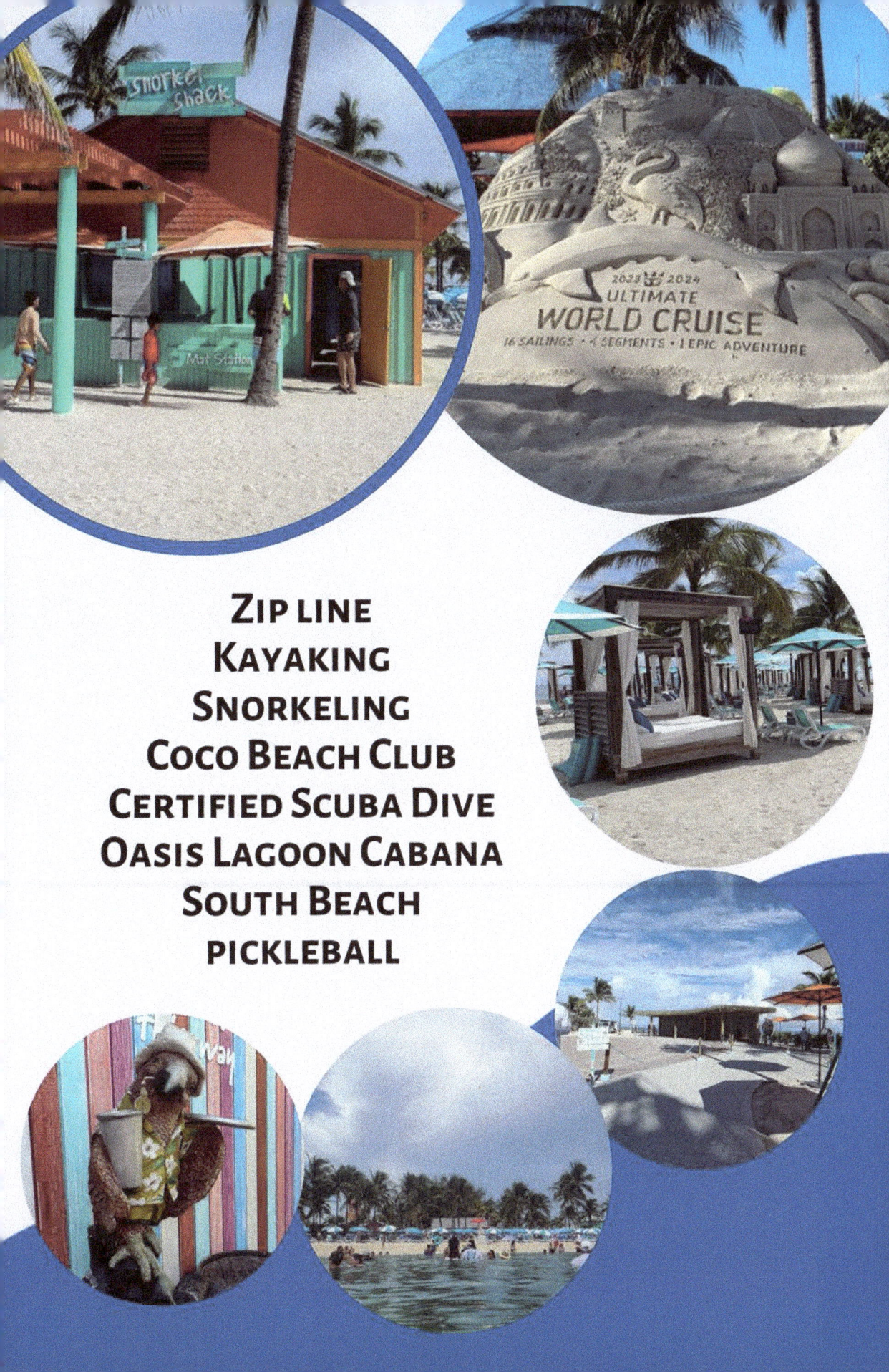

Zip line
Kayaking
Snorkeling
Coco Beach Club
Certified Scuba Dive
Oasis Lagoon Cabana
South Beach
pickleball

ACTIVITIES & FOOD

SPLASH SUMMIT   CHILL GRILL
DAREDEVIL'S TOWER   SLICE OF PARADISE
WAVEPOOL   SWIM-UP BAR
CHILL ISLAND   SKIPPER'S GRILL
OVERWATER CABANAS   CAPTAIN JACK'S
SPLASHAWAY BAY   SNACKSHACK
UP UP AND AWAY
AND MORE!

MOST OF THE FREE ACTIVITIES AND FOOD ARE
NEAR THE DOCK.

Arrivals Plaza is your starting point. You can do free activities at a few places such as Sports Court, Captain Jill's Galleon for children, Splashaway Bay, Chill Island, Oasis Lagoon, Harbor Beach, and South Beach,

BREAKFAST ISN'T AVAILABLE ON THE ISLAND. YOU HAVE UNTIL BEFORE 5PM DEPARTURE TIME TO ENJOY THE ISLAND. YOU CAN DO ALL DAY SNORKELING. YOU NEED TO PICK UP THE SNORKELING GEAR FOR YOUR ALL DAY SNORKELING EXCURSION AT SNORKEL SHACK AT CHILL ISLAND. IT IS 5-10 MINUTES WALK FROM THE ARRIVALS PLAZA AND TO THE LEFT SIDE OF THE ISLAND. KEEP THE GEAR WITH YOU. IT IS HARDER TO GET YOUR SIZE LATER ON. YOU SHOULD PICK UP ON TIME. RETURN IT BACK TO THE SAME LOCATION. IT IS WISE TO BE EARLY ON THE ISLAND OR TO GO THERE LATER IN THE AFTERNOON WHEN THERE ARE FEWER PEOPLE. THE WEATHER WILL BE BETTER. THERE ARE MANY BEACHES AVAILABLE, BUT THE ONES FURTHER AWAY HAVE FEWER PEOPLE SUCH AS SOUTH BEACH. YOU CAN TAKE THE TRAM THERE. YOU CAN ENJOY SWIMMING IN THE POOL. THEY HAVE VIDEOS TO GIVE YOU TIPS BEFORE YOU COME HERE. CAPTAIN JACK'S HAS AN ALA CARTE MENU. YOU CAN EAT AND DRINK AS MUCH AS YOU LIKE AT THE COMPLIMENTARY RESTAURANTS. YOUR SEAPASS IS REQUIRED TO ACCESS THE PAID AREAS. THE ZIPLINE HAS

THREE TOWERS. THEY HAVE YOU CLIMB UP EACH ONE AFTER ARRIVAL. TAKING PHOTOS AND VIDEOS CAN ONLY DONE AT THE THIRD TOWER. THEY WILL DELAY IF THERE ARE WEATHER ISSUES. YOU CAN GO ALL AROUND THE ISLAND AND IT WILL LAND AT HARBOR BEACH. IT IS A 5-10 MINUTE WALK BACK TO THE START. YOU SHOULD HAVE WALKIE TALKIES IF YOU ARE TRAVELING AS A GROUP TO COMMUNICATE IF YOU DON'T HAVE AN INTERNET PACKAGE. INTERNET WORKS HERE IF YOU HAVE THE PACKAGE. YOUR DRINK PACKAGE CAN BE USED ON THE ISLAND. THEY HAVE TOWELS, LOCKERS, SHOWERS, CHAIRS FOR FREE TO USE. TRAVEL LIGHT, BUT TAKE YOUR CAMERA AND PHONE WITH YOU. THEY HAVE A NATURE TRAIL TO EXPLORE AND SO MUCH MORE. THERE ARE LESS PEOPLE ON THE ISLAND AT 2PM. YOU HAVE THE FLEXIBILITY TO GO BACK TO THE CRUISE SHIP OR STAY THERE IF YOU HAVEN'T BOOKED EXCURSIONS IN THE MORNING. YOU CAN ENJOY THE QUIETER BEACHES FURTHER AWAY FROM THE ENTRANCE. YOU CAN RIDE THE TRAM TO DIFFERENT PARTS OF THE ISLAND TO START

YOUR DAY AFTER YOU GET PAST THE ARRIVAL AREA. THERE WERE LADIES DRESSED IN CARIBBEAN STYLE COSTUMES ON THE ISLAND TO GREET TOURISTS. YOU WILL ALWAYS FIND PHOTOGRAPHERS ON THE SHIP AND ON THE ISLAND LOOKING FOR A CHANCE TO TAKE PHOTOS FOR YOU AT A COST. YOU CAN ALSO ENJOY COMPLIMENTARY ICE CREAM AT A FEW RESTAURANTS ON THE ISLAND. THE PHOTOS ARE MOSTLY FROM THE CHILL ISLAND SECTION OF THE ISLAND. THERE ARE PHOTOS OF SOME OTHER PARTS OF THE ISLAND. PLAN WHERE YOU WANT TO GO. THE STARTING POINT OF THE SNORKELING IS AWAY FROM CHILL GRILL AND THE TRAM STOP. THE TRAM IS YOUR BEST OPTION BUT YOU TO SCHEDULE WHEN TO VISIT DIFFERENT PARTS OF THE ISLAND.

Chill Grill

✳ Daily Food Memo ✳

THERE ARE A FEW OPTIONS FOR COMPLIMENTARY FOOD AT COCOCAY. YOU CAN CHECK OUT THESE RESTAURANTS AND EAT FOR FREE: SKIPPER'S GRILL, CAPTAIN JACK'S, CHILL GRILL, AND SNACK SHACK. CAPTAIN JACK'S IS ACROSS FROM SKIPPER'S GRILL IT IS OFFERS AL LA CARTE DINING. IT IS THE MAIN RESTAURANT FOR A VARIETY OF FOOD. CHILL GRILL IS THE LARGEST RESTAURANT ON THE ISLAND WITH THE MOST OPTIONS. SNACK SHACK IS THE MOST ACCESSIBLE WITH THREE DIFFERENT LOCATIONS AT THRILL WATERPARK, ONE NEAR OASIS LAGOON, AND ONE ON SOUTH BEACH. THE OTHER RESTAURANTS HAVE A FEE. BEVERAGES MAY NOT BE INCLUDED UNLESS YOU HAVE A BEVERAGE PACKAGE THAT YOU PURCHASED AND USED ON THE CRUISE. THEY CHARGE PER DAY. IT IS BETTER TO GET PURCHASE THESE WHEN THEY ARE ON SALE PRIOR TO BOARDING THE CRUISE. ALL NEW CHARGES WILL GO TO YOUR SEAPASS. IT IS MORE EXPENSIVE THEN.

COCOCAY

Up, Up and Away

SPORTS PAVILLON

WHILE RIDING THE TRAM

THIRD ZIPLINE TOWER

WILD IGUANA AND CHICKENS

BLACK CRAB

HIDEAWAY BEACH

Enjoy a private adult only beach. This is a great place to spend away for the children. You need to pay to use the facilities here, but they have a hut with free food complimentary for those on the Royal Caribbean cruise, but double check to find out if it is free. Their Blog channel gives you helpful information that they won't tell you on the cruise.

It is for adults who are at least 18 years old. The complimentary tram service can take you there. It is a short five-minute walk. It has an infinity pool and cabanas. There are chairs and umbrellas, palapas, hammocks, day beds, resort-style loungers, and swings. It also has a swim-up bar with a DJ. There are two restaurants that are complimentary. It is the only place you can get shrimp, fish, and ceviche. You can get pizza and freshly made empanadas from Slice of Paradise. You can get food delivered to you at your cabana if you booked one. Drinks are an additional cost, so it's better to have a beverage package purchased earlier on that you can use on the cruise and on the island. You can also enjoy free non-alcoholic beverages at the buffet and Cafe Promenade. You need to have the ship Wi-Fi for communication with your party and the ship staff, but sometimes the network is down to stay connected if you separate.

If you are willing to purchase a package for Coco Beach Club, you can enjoy herb-marinated filet mignon or grilled Bahamian lobster with nice craft cocktails. Make sure you can enjoy the rum-soaked cake.

DINNER AT MAIN DINING

Final Night Show

Elisa Furr singing
tribute to Celion Dion

You are requested to leave your room by 9AM or so with your belongings. If you ask Guest Services, they will tell you a time. You automatically get checked out. They want you to go to the assigned deck based on the group number shown on the app when you depart the ship. They will make sure everyone is off the ship because they are expecting the next group of people to board the ship at 11:30AM. They need a few hours to prepare for the ship for those travelers.

Reminder

On the last night on board the cruise, You will get the bill from Royal Caribbean. Double check it and settle any discrepancies tonight. It is hard to fix it once you leave the cruise. You need to pack your belongings into your checked baggage and carryon luggage. The cruise line will give you luggage tags on the last night of the cruise. You must put on your luggage and leave it outside your cabin for them to pick up. Keep to set aside clothes to wear the next day. Make room for packing your pajamas and remaining items that you need for the last night and next morning. Your personal item should hold your boarding pass, passport, wallet etc that you needed the first day traveling. Keep electronics in the personal bag. Double check that everything is packed. You won't be able to access the carryon and checked bag if you tag it and leave it outside your room. Set your alarm if you need to. Check the time it must be outside your stateroom. You will need to claim it at the airport.

Make sure you know when to be at the airport and you arranged your ride to get there. Remember to catch the shuttle bus transit to get back to the airport. You would have to arrange this. If you took the VIA Rail train, you will need to be prepared to get to the station immediately after landing in Canada at Pearson Airport. If you took the train to Windsor, then you need to leave Detroit immediately. If you have the time, it is better to allow an extra day of vacation to avoid any delays or missing your train. You also have to remember it takes time to cross the Detroit border to get back to Windsor. There could be delays especially on weekends.

BACK AT FT. LAUDERDALE

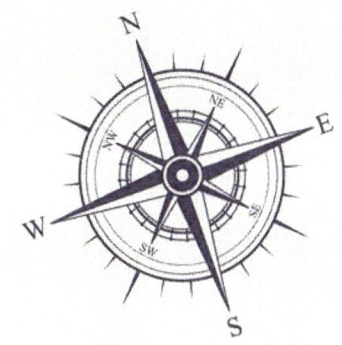

ROYAL CARIBBEAN WANTS YOU OUT OF YOUR CABIN BY 8:00AM OR 9:00AM. THEY WANT PEOPLE OUT BY 9:20AM. IF YOU HAVE MORE THAN 3 HOURS, YOU CAN SPEND TIME HERE. PLAN YOUR TIME WISELY. YOU MAY WANT TO DISEMBARK EARLIER. THERE WILL BE A LOT OF PEOPLE WAITING FOR A TAXI OR SHUTTLE.

BREAK FAST

You can get a quick breakfast on the ship. Cafe Promenade is a great place for quick breakfast. Breakfast is served as early as 7:00AM in the main dining room. You will have to check your boarding pass for your flight. It's nice to have food to eat on the flight home. Otherwise, you need to buy lunch at the airport. If you booked afternoon, you may want to eat before your flight.

Its best to disembark as soon as you can. Self assist disembarkation can be done. You need to carry all your luggage with you. You can change your luggage tags if you don't like it. There is nothing to do on the ship. Plan your time wisely when to leave. Let them know when you leave. It's best not to wait for them to call you. You can give yourself more time if you disembark early. Remember you will have delays if you leave the ship later. Make sure you have plenty of time before your flight and to avoid long security checking lines. You might be able to get a standby flight to arrive home earlier. You need to avoid any additional delays traveling. Port Everglades is close to the airport. You need to go through security and deal with traffic delays when you leave later. Make sure you arrive early at the airport. Shuttle bus and taxi can also get delayed arriving to the airport.

Travel home safely!

Ft. Lauderdale, Florida is known to have lightning strikes and weather conditions that affect flights. Your flight could be delayed by a few hours. If you need to cross the border from Detroit to Windsor, you will have to consider possible delays arriving at the border and crossing over whether its the bridge or the tunnel. An afternoon flight, may become a night arrival home. An evening flight, can become delayed to night flight and later night to midnight arrival. The flight attendant may also request you to get your baggage labeled due to the shortage of shortage space for carryon baggage.

If you are sensitive to cold, wear your jacket on the plane and turn off the air conditioner. It is easy for germs to pass on the flight. It is recommended to wear a mask to protect yourself. The cold air conditioning and Hot weather outside during the vacation also can affect your health especially if you had sunburn. You will still feel the heat and pain. Mine lasted beyond the length of this vacation.

At Detroit Metro Airport, everyone is in a hurry to gather their luggage from the baggage claim on Level 1. You need to proceed back to Level 2 if you want the shuttle, taxi, or Uber. Allow enough time for the shuttle or whatever service you called to arrive at the airport. There are various shuttles from different hotels that come to pick up passengers aside from the airport parking shuttles. That day was busy when waiting for the shuttle bus to arrive from the specific hotel chain. They should take your luggage for you into the trunk. Some of these drivers require you to give them full instructions. One Uber driver parked away from where they were told and made us have to walk over with the luggage. He said that there are too many people and vehicles he couldn't park there. The shuttle bus was going to leave without checking to see if there were additional passengers and luggage to take. Make you have all your receipts for your purchases on hand to claim when the border officer asks. They know that tourists buy rum and coffee in Jamaica.

.

Enjoy your vacation!

REFERENCES

Royal Caribbean, "Shore Excursions"
Royal Caribbean, 2024.
https://www.royalcaribbean.com/booked/shore-excursions

Visit Florida, "City of Fort Lauderdale" Visit Florida, 2024.
https://www.visitflorida.com/places-to-go/southeast/fort-lauderdale/

Cayman Islands, "Tours & Adventures" Cayman Islands, 2024.
https://www.visitcaymanislands.com/en-us/things-to-do/tours-adventures

Royal Caribbean, "George Town, Grand Cayman" Royal Caribbean, 2024.
https://www.royalcaribbean.com/cruise-to/george-town-grand-cayman

Royal Caribbean, "What to do in Falmouth, Jamaica" Royal Caribbean, June 5, 2020.
https://www.royalcaribbean.com/blog/inside-look-what-to-do-in-falmouth-jamaica/

John Shallo, "Best Things to do in Falmouth, Jamaica" Cruise Addicts, October 29, 2023.
https://cruiseaddicts.com/best-things-to-do-in-falmouth-jamaica/

REFERENCES

Royal Caribbean, "Nassau, Bahamas"
Royal Caribbean, 2024.
https://www.royalcaribbean.com/cruise-to/nassau-bahamas

Royal Caribbean, "CocoCay Cruises"
Royal Caribbean, 2024.
https://www.royalcaribbean.com/cococay-cruises

Royal Caribbean, "Free things to do at Perfect Day at CocoCay" Royal Caribbean, 2024.
https://www.royalcaribbean.com/guides/free-things-to-do-at-perfect-day-at-cococay

Royal Caribbean, "Best Restaurants at Perfect Day at CocoCay" Royal Caribbean, 2024.
https://www.royalcaribbean.com/guides/best-restaurants-at-perfect-day-at-cococay

Matt Hochberg, "Hideaway Beach at CocoCay: cost, tips & review" Royal Caribbean, 2010-2024.
https://www.royalcaribbeanblog.com/hideaway-beach-adults-only

Royal Caribbean, "Hideaway Beach"
Royal Caribbean, 2024.
https://www.royalcaribbean.com/perfect-day-cococay/hideaway-beach

OTHER PRODUCTS

Knowing God

How to Hear God's Voice

New Life in Jesus

Loving Israel

God's Gifts

Meeting God

Word Power

Fruit of the Spirit

The Tabernacle

Bride for Jesus

A Life of Prayer

Live Free

Who am I in Jesus

Walk in Love

God's Favor

Man of God

Woman of God

How to Use Money

God's Wisdom

Fasting

See Jerusalem and Bethany

First Fruit Offering

Feast of Trumpets

Day of Atonement

Feast of Tabernacles

Counting the Omer

Festival of Lights

Glory, Presence, and Holy Spirit

Live in God's Presence

How God Speaks

Knowing Jesus

Knowing Holy Spirit

A Healthy Life

Healthy Life Work Book

Smokey the Cat

Passover Unleavened Bread

Resurrection Life

The Blessing

Revival

Chelsea Learns Hebrew

Give Thanks

Thanksgiving

Jesus' Birth

Proverbs 31 Woman

Loving Jesus: Bride and Groom

Colours in the Bible

Breakthroughs

Open Doors

The Seven Spirits of God

OTHER PRODUCTS

Numbers in the Bible

Aglee the Eagle

An Eagle's Life

ABC's of Faith

Angels

Chelsea Learns Numbers in

Hebrew

Feast of Purim

A Royal Life

Family Day

Family Blessings

Chinese New Year

Worship

Pandas

Canada

Celia's Birthday

Animal Stories

Eagles

Coming Soon

Travel West Caribbean

Chelsea Psalms and Poems 3

Fun in West Caribbean

Puzzle Books

Biblical Puzzle Book Volume 1-5

Bible Puzzles for Young Children Book 1-3

Biblical Puzzle for Children Books 1-5

Chelsea's Bible Puzzles

Devotionals

31 Day Devotional

Inspirational/Other

Chelsea's Psalms and Poems

Your Daily Meal: Chelsea's Food Album

Chelsea's Psalms and Poems2

Teaching Series

How to Hear God's Voice Teaching Guide & Audio Book

Relationship with God, Jesus, Holy Spirit Guide

Knowing God, Jesus, Holy Spirit Guide & Audio Book

Flowing in the Prophetic

Teaching (Non-Sale on the website)

Purim

Passover

Resurrection

More books to come!

OTHER PRODUCTS

Coming soon

Angels

Chelsea Learns Numbers in
Hebrew

More books on Amazon, Kobo, and
Barnes and Noble, and Smashwords.
https://chelseak532002550.wordpress.com/

More books on Amazon, Kobo, Barnes and Noble,
and Smashwords.
https://www.amazon.com/author/chelseakong

Please leave a review to help the author
continue to write more books to reach more
readers. Thank you so much for your support.

Review!

About
CHELSEA KONG

She is a writer, creative arts and digital media artist, skilled administration and certified PCP (Payroll Compliance Professional), and podcaster. Chelsea also served in a variety of roles, from audiovisual, photography, to assisting on the worship team, and ministry team. She also has a passion for families being united.

Chelsea has been a guest on Unity Live Radio, The Lady Tracey Show, and How to Live for Christ and is highly recommended by a Proud Christian blog. She is also a guest blogger. A few of her books have been featured in YourAuthorHub, etc. She a diploma in Hotel and Restaurant Management, Digital Media Arts, Office Administration, and she is certified as a Payroll Compliance Professional, and experience working with children. Chelsea lives in Toronto, Canada. She mainly writes children's books, stories, bridal writing, poems, lyrics for songs, words of encouragement, blessings, prayers, and jokes. The author of How to Hear the Voice of God, the Bridal Collection, Knowing God, etc. She also has her own Bible Puzzle books and other inspired products. Her podcast channel is called Chelsea K on Anchor, Spotify, and iTunes.

Please check my website to find out more:
https://chelseak532002550.wordpress.com/

www.ingramcontent.com/pod-product-compliance
Lightning Source LLC
Chambersburg PA
CBHW041137120626
46547CB00020B/3025